W9-CMG-846

GREEK POLITICS
AT A CROSSROADS

HOOVER INTERNATIONAL STUDIES
Peter Duignan, general editor

Publications in the Hoover International Studies series of the Hoover Institution on War, Revolution and Peace are concerned with U.S. involvement in world and regional politics. These studies are intended to represent a contribution to the discussion and debate of major questions of international affairs.

GREEK POLITICS AT A CROSSROADS

What Kind of Socialism?

Roy C. Macridis

HOOVER INSTITUTION PRESS
Stanford University | Stanford, California

The Hoover Institution on War, Revolution and Peace, founded at Stanford University in 1919 by the late President Herbert Hoover, is an interdisciplinary research center for advanced study on domestic and international affairs in the twentieth century. The views expressed in its publications are entirely those of the authors and do not necessarily reflect the views of the staff, officers, or Board of Overseers of the Hoover Institution.

Hoover Press Publication 299

Copyright 1984 by the Board of Trustees of the
    Leland Stanford Junior University

First printing, 1984
Manufactured in the United States of America
88 87 86 85 84   9 8 7 6 5 4 3 2 1

Library of Congress Cataloging in Publication Data
Macridis, Roy C.
    Greek politics at a crossroads.

    (Hoover international studies)
    Bibliography: p.
    1. Socialism—Greece. 2. Communism—Greece. 3. Greece—Politics and government—1974–
I. Title. II. Series.
HX375.5.A6M32   1984   949.5′076   84–3772
ISBN 0–8179–7992–1

Contents

Tables

Editor's Foreword

In this policy study Professor Roy C. Macridis seeks to answer the question: Whither Greek socialism? He analyzes Greece under Andreas Papandreou since 1981 and discusses the nature of the newly established socialist Greek state. According to Macridis, the Panhellenic Socialist Movement (PASOK) led by Papandreou can travel one of two roads. Like Mitterrand in France, it can follow the Western model (democratic socialism, observance of civil liberties and processes and decentralization with more worker participation), with a firm commitment to Europe and to the Western Alliance. If this policy is followed, PASOK will become a centrist or reformist party supported by most of the Greek middle class.

The second road will take Greece in the direction of socialism of a Third World kind, that is, a single-party dictatorship. PASOK will seek to control all levels of government and will radicalize the bureaucracy. Moving toward one-party governance means rejecting the Western socialist model and joining the so-called neutralist camp. PASOK's dominant themes will be nationalist, anti-American, and anti-Turk; it will call for independence from NATO and the Common Market. Efforts will be made, therefore, to dissociate Greece from the United States and the Western Alliance. Opposition groups will be suppressed, and Greece, the founder of democracy, will become a Third World one-party dictatorship. The costs of these policies to Greeks in terms of freedom and economic efficiency will be high. The Communist Party of Greece is not likely to accept these changes peacefully, so the threat of civil war will be great.

American interests are not well served if PASOK makes Greece into a Third World dictatorship. For the United States, a Greece committed to NATO, the Western Alliance, and a form of Western socialism is much to be preferred. Greece (and Turkey) are strategically important to the United States and its NATO allies. NATO cannot defend the eastern Mediterranean without the help of both Greece and Turkey, who are hostile allies. Greece and Turkey are valuable to NATO for the bases and facilities they provide, and for the air, naval, and ground forces they command.

If PASOK pursues a nationalistic, independent path that is neutralist, independent of NATO and the Common Market, and anti-Turk, the United States and NATO will lose control of the eastern Mediterranean and will not be able to defend Turkey from the Soviets. Neither Greece nor Turkey can defend itself against a Soviet threat, hence the terrible dilemma facing the United States. The United States has little or no influence on internal Greek affairs. We can only hope Papandreou and PASOK will follow the road of Western socialism. But through aid and diplomacy, the United States can encourage Greek and Turk alike at least to arrive at a peaceful solution to their disputes. Here too, however, the United States is threatened by PASOK's ultranationalism and anti-Turkish rhetoric. This critical situation is clearly analyzed and described in a balanced fashion in Professor Macridis's excellent monograph.

Peter Duignan

Coordinator, International Studies
Hoover Institution

Preface

What are the prospects for democracy in Greece? Will the socialist party (PASOK) that won the election in 1981 follow the Western model or will it move in the direction of Third World one-party regimes or even Latin American authoritarianism? This study is addressed to these questions.

There are powerful international and domestic forces that may keep Greece within the Western world as a democracy; but there are equally strong pulls in the direction of the Third World populist movements, as the growing strength of the Communist Party of Greece—the only communist party that has been gaining strength in Europe—attests. The present socialist leaders seem caught between the two forces pulling them in two different directions and the future course they will take remains uncertain. A great deal hangs in the balance. The foreign policy and the alliances of this small, strategically located country, will ultimately be determined by the intensity and divisiveness of the domestic political discourse and the way in which powerful conflicting ideologies and pent-up emotions are resolved.

I have tried to suggest some tentative hypotheses and discuss them in the context of recent political developments in the southern Mediterranean, where socialist parties and movements have been gaining but where socialism has its own particular and special traits and national imperatives.

I want to thank my colleague and friend, Seymour M. Lipset, for first encouraging me to do this study. My warmest thanks also go to Peter Duignan for his friendly interest and to Richard T. Burress, who kept in touch with me on behalf of the Hoover Institution. To the fellows and directors of the Hoover Institution I am much obliged for the financial help they gave me to travel to Greece on two occasions. As for my Greek colleagues and the various political leaders I talked with, they are too many to be mentioned here. I want to thank each and all for the many conversations we had, and I hope we shall continue to have, on Greek politics—just as much a staple commodity in Greece at lunch or dinner as olives and feta. None of them are even remotely responsible for the thoughts I express in this study. Last, I want to thank Geri Spaulding for her help in typing the manuscript.

1 | Introduction

The countries of Southern Europe have been going through a process of rapid modernization with all its concomitant hopes, realizations, and dislocations. Urbanization has spread rapidly, so much so that as Juan Linz puts it, the ancient lands of the *polis* are now the countries of huge sprawling megalopolises where millions of "urban villagers" live in varying degrees of squalor.[1] Economic growth and modernization have been rapid in Spain, Italy, and Greece. Per capita income has tripled in 40 years, and the number of farmers among those gainfully employed has dropped sharply. Some of the amenities of modernity—health care, transportation, leisure, education, and entertainment—have been made available to many, satisfying some needs and whetting appetites for more. Generally, "want formation" has exceeded "want satisfaction."[2]

Politically, throughout Southern Europe and particularly in Greece, the impact of economic growth has been rapid and highly destabilizing because it came too late (after the end of World War II). It undermined rigid political and social oligarchies, forcing them to acquiesce to the development of participatory mechanisms and institutions, such as national and mass parties. Democracy returned in Portugal, Spain, and even in Greece, only in the early 1970s. The authoritarian structures that provided the governance of Greece before 1974, even if behind the facade of a democracy or through the military junta (1967–1974), broke. They were replaced by a democratic constitution, individual freedoms, free elections, associational and party freedoms, and in general by a degree of pluralism that Greece (Portugal and Spain as well) had not experienced in the past. However, the momentum and weight of political participation that had been stalled for so long made the newly established democratic institutions fragile and uncertain. The new groups that entered the political stage often did so in the name of intransigent and total ideologies aimed at subordinating and, if possible, eliminating the groups that comprised the oligarchy: the church, the army, the upper middle classes, the landed aristocracy and notables, and various state agencies—notably the bureaucracy —the so-called establishment. The result has been an ongoing crisis of legitimacy—an uncertainty about the rules according to which conflict and political competition can be resolved, a suspicion of pluralism, and a constant yearning for authoritarian solutions from the left or the right.

The crisis of legitimacy becomes even more acute because of modernization and economic growth. Samuel P. Huntington made the point some time ago. He emphasized the destabilizing effect of the constant growth of demands and expectations on fragile institutional structures. The "praetorian politics" model applied to many developing countries until the recession of the 1970s.[3] Equally and perhaps even more destabilizing since then, however, has been the sudden arrest of economic growth and the lowering of the standard of living. The tensions of economic growth and modernization become revolutionary when suddenly not only the hope for more wanes but when economic stagnation threatens both income and the newly attained status.[4] Similarly, the political ideologies developed by groups, who earlier asked for and received greater satisfaction of their demands, gain in intensity. Relative deprivation becomes, indeed, an even more potent revolutionary force. Ideologies increasingly become weapons pointed at the establishment; they mobilize and activate disparate groups of the citizenry. They are often couched in transcendental terms that promise to transform radically the existing political, social, and economic landscape.

Populist movements in the name of communitarianism and nationalism gain momentum. Populist ideologies, however, set forth new horizons of wellbeing and satisfaction that cannot be easily attained. Demands, long dormant, appear like impulsive dreams seeking immediate fulfillment. They have to be harnessed and controlled. Satisfaction must be deferred. This may be one reason why most populist movements in so many countries give place to authoritarian and repressive policies and regimes, in which the leadership spawned by revolutionary ideologies imposes controls to maintain itself in power or arrest the constant turmoil in the society that they engender. There is no permanent revolution. On the contrary, most populist revolutions, even those in the name of socialism, give place to repressive authoritarian regimes that harness and direct economic growth and development through economic planning, austerity, and discipline. The state, the bureaucracy, and the military become the agencies that replace the old oligarchy. Support is shaped and manipulated through the inculcation of nationalist ideologies or through a mass single party.

This study explores the nature and the fragility of the newly established democratic institutions and discusses the character, organization, and ideology of the recently founded (1974) Panhellenic Socialist Movement (PASOK) that won the election of 1981. PASOK challenged the establishment; it promised national independence and socialism. In many respects, it was like many of the socialist movements that developed in Third World countries after World War II. But in other respects, it identified with socialist parties and movements of the West, claiming to be attached to democracy and pluralism.

The central hypothesis of this study is that the leadership of PASOK is likely to follow one of two different courses. The first will be in the direction of what might be called the Western socialist model, an attachment to civil liberties and democratic processes within the framework of the existing constitution established in 1974 and scrupulously adhered to until now. It is the kind of democratic socialism that will entail selective socialization, in such areas as heavy industry, trade, and insurance; restructuring of the administrative machinery of the state through decentralization; increased participation of workers, farmers, and others in the management and direction of their enterprises, farms, and other units of production and administration; and comprehensive reforms in education. Modernization will be geared to national needs and imperatives, and every effort will be made to limit the direct impact of outside intervention and alleviate the country's dependence on foreign (especially U.S.) help. As with the Mitterrand Socialists, national considerations will play an important role but by and large Greece will remain (with qualifications and reservations) within Europe and the Atlantic Alliance but with every effort made to diversify its alliances and the sources of support, aid, and military procurement. PASOK will increasingly move in the direction of the center, from which it derived a major part of its electoral support, to become a reformist party and will continue to draw strength from the enlightened elements of the middle classes.

The second course that merits special attention is one that will see Greece move progressively in the direction of the Third World model of socialism. It will move the country in substance, if not in form, in the direction of a single-party state. PASOK and its leadership will attempt to consolidate their position by infiltrating and controlling the local units of government (and here decentralization will make the job easier) and by neutralizing, purging, and ultimately gaining control of the top decision-making centers (the only office now beyond their reach is the presidency of the republic). Important changes in the personnel of the key ministries, Interior, Justice, and Defense, will take place. With or without decentralization, radical personnel changes will be undertaken at the municipalitiy and department (*nomos*) levels. In other words, there will be a convergent strategy directed at both the top and the base. Similarly, how PASOK organizes workers and farmers in industries and in the cooperatives, and the role they will be asked to play in managing firms and cooperatives will give another important indication of PASOK's infiltration and control.

The possibility that PASOK may move in the direction of Third World socialism has a direct bearing on foreign policy and strategy. For, inevitably, if PASOK moves in the direction of one-party governance, it will do so by rejecting the Western model of socialist democratic government; it will also insist on independence and nonalignment along the lines of the Third World model. The new leadership will rationalize its policies in terms of the national imperatives of security against Turkey; the uncertainties of U.S. help and support; the inadmissibility of the presence of foreign forces in Greece; the incompatibilities between the pro-Israel, but also pro-Turkish, stance of the United States; and the interests of Greece in the Arab world (what Papandreou calls the "Arab nation"). It will also reject economic penetration by the United States and Western Europe and dissociate itself from the Atlantic Alliance and the Common Market. Nationalism will provide political and mass support and legitimize PASOK's efforts to control the base and the state apparatus until it silences opposition.

There are a number of forces that will obviously resist PASOK's efforts, and they must be taken into consideration. The first is, surprisingly enough, the Communist Party of Greece. It is particularly sensitive to PASOK's efforts to widen its popular base in cities, rural areas, and among farmers, workers, and students. Communist party moves and tactics indicate a great deal about the moves PASOK's militants are making and reveal a great deal about PASOK's tactics. The second group to resist will be the various notables associated with the former majority party, Nea Democratia. They are the first to feel the political squeeze both at the local level (such as the drying out of patronage or control by popular committees) and at the national level (dismissals, replacements, early retirements) and to sense that they are being neutralized and about to be set aside. Third, the various administrative bodies—the civil service, the university professorial corps, the judiciary, and high-ranking army officers—will resist purges, and again their reaction will clearly show the degree and extent of the attempted purge or their acquiescence. The same is true of police and security forces. Last, the office of the president of the republic and his immediate associates, who are not now controlled by PASOK, will be particularly sensitive to any efforts to undermine their office or to control it when a new president is elected sometime in June 1985.

The most important single variable, however, is the Communist Party of Greece. If it grows stronger—and there is every indication that it will—it becomes a powerful constraint on PASOK's attempts to establish single-party governance without an alliance with the Communists. Given the nature of PASOK as a populist party, the prospects of its moving to the center and even to the right to establish an authoritarian system with the help of the middle classes, the bureaucracy, and even the military should be entertained seriously. Similarly, the use of foreign policy—that is, the manipulation of international issues, notably the relations between Greece and Turkey—may provide PASOK and its leadership with both the pretext and the support for the establishment of an authoritarian regime. Finally, the position of the conservative opposition party (Nea Democratia) will be a significant factor. If it remains disorganized and without strong leadership, PASOK's leader could more easily impose a one-party system.

In the first chapter, I suggest a theoretical framework to distinguish Western democratic socialism from Third World socialist parties and regimes—what may be termed "authoritarian socialism." I differentiate also between two types or phases of authoritarian socialism—single-party socialism as distinguished from state, bureaucratic, or even military socialism. In chapter 2, I give an overview of electoral and party politics as they evolved in Greece between World War II and August 1974, when the military junta fell. I then examine in some detail the crucial election of October 1981, which PASOK won. Was it a critical election representing a realignment of political parties and forces in democratic politics or a protest vote with all the earmarks of a populist movement? Finally, I examine the current trends in the evolution of PASOK. Is it moving in the direction of democratic socialism or is it gradually assuming the authoritarian stance of Third World socialist movements and regimes? What is the record of the socialist government that took office in October 1981?

2 | Democratic and Authoritarian Socialism

The Determining Factors

My main purpose here is to distinguish as clearly as possible democratic socialist movements and regimes (mostly in Western Europe) from Third World socialist movements, with one central question always in mind: Where does the Greek socialist movement belong? I intend also to distinguish two phases in the development of authoritarian socialism: the populist phase, primarily targeted at the acquisition of political power, and the regime consolidation phase, primarily related to the maintenance of power and the legitimization of the new regime.[1]

Little need be said about the underlying ideology, organization, and policies of Western socialist movements and parties.[2] They have been, by and large but with serious qualifications and pauses, committed to socialism. They advocate economic planning, nationalization, comprehensive welfare measures, and income redistribution. The pace of social and economic structural reforms and the institutional mechanisms through which they are implemented vary. There have been noticeably long pauses in some countries—for instance, in Western Germany and England—and there have been heart-rending reexaminations of the gospel of nationalization among almost all socialist parties except the French, which did not win a majority in an election until 1981.

The Western socialist parties (excluding Mediterranean Europe) accepted the tenets of democracy: party pluralism, the rights of the opposition, individual freedoms, freedom of the press, freedom of association, and a commitment to government "alternance"—the understanding that the opposition will form the new government if it wins in a free election. These principles were accepted well before the advent of Leninism and the formation of communist parties that adhered to the 21 conditions of the Third International. It is my contention that it is this commitment to democracy, rather than the economic and social philosophy and structural reforms they propose to carry out, that distinguishes Western socialism from all other forms of socialism. Western socialism remains attached to democracy and pluralism and seeks to implement all its economic and societal programs through open debate, persuasion, and free elections.

Most other socialist movements and regimes, particularly those that have emerged in Third World countries, have moved in an authoritarian direction. In almost all of them, authoritarianism has assumed one of three forms of organizational and political control—single-party, statist-bureaucratic, and military—with various combinations of the three.

Whether socialism is to be democratic (following the Western model) or authoritarian (whatever particular form of authoritarianism it may assume) depends on a number of considerations. Foremost is the political culture of the given country, its level of economic development and modernization, and its relative degree of independence or dependence on the world economy. These considerations are of particular significance for the study of socialism in Greece and in other countries of Mediterranean Europe.

Political Culture

The term is used to denote the complex of attitudes and orientations people have toward their political regime, their government, and its policies. It is also used to indicate the levels of support that the political regime enjoys, the degree of political integration and of political participation, and the manner in which individuals view themselves in the political system—the roles they play and the roles they think they can play.[3]

In regimes where participation has been relatively high and a sense of citizenship widespread, and where the state and the government have been viewed as agencies for the realization of interests, demands, and aspirations, Western socialist parties and socialist governments have emerged in open and democratic political cultures. Socialist parties have been mass parties closely identified with workers and trade unions. Over a period of time, they have developed open and democratic internal structures—even if, as Michels pointed out, the elite played and continues to play a dominant role. Internal freedom and persuasion have been intimately related to rank-and-file support. Socialist parties became fully legitimized within the political system and were accepted even by those opposed to the principles they embody. They became coherent, stable, and legitimized organizations operating within a coherent, stable, and legitimized political regime.

In the absence of such a political culture, one that we associate with Western Europe, the Scandinavian countries, England, some English-speaking former colonies, and the United States, socialist movements and parties, whether aspiring to power or in power, have developed different characteristics. They have attempted to do far more than what political parties in general and socialist parties in particular are expected to do in Western democracies. Instead of specific social, economic, or political policy goals, they aspire to universal goals—national independence and nation-building; rapid political mobilization within the society; and radical overhaul of the social structure and the political institutions in order to establish a new political regime. Their ideology becomes all-inclusive. They try also to cut across classes and social and ethnic groups by espousing unifying social and national themes. Since political regimes had not yet been shaped and legitimized in Third World countries, the indigenous socialist movements attempted to refashion them. They did not operate within a constitution but often opposed it. They did not accept existing political formulas but proposed new ones. All Third World socialist parties therefore took an inherently radical and revolutionary stance.

Economic Development

The level of economic development in any given country is the second most important factor in fashioning the ideology and shaping the policies of socialist movements. It may be argued that it was Eduard Bernstein and not Marx who diagnosed better the evolution of modern (Western) capitalism and provided the proper prescriptions for the strategy and tactics of socialist parties and movements as they developed in the West. Liberal Western capitalism generated many of the institutions without which socialist parties and governments could not have developed. Among them are national political parties, representative assemblies, universal franchise, trade unionism, and public education. Socioeconomic developments and associational freedoms aided the growth of socialism; trade unions, a highly differentiated working class, a burgeoning white-collar and salaried middle class, and above all relative prosperity and welfare legislation sharply mitigated the class conflict that the Marxists had predicted and with it the need for a revolutionary seizure of power. Instead, everywhere in the West socialism was evolutionary and a matter of persuasion and political choice.

It is generally in the less economically developed societies that authoritarianism and authoritarian forms of socialism have emerged. Many of these countries are still backward. They lack capital for industrialization, investments in the extractive industries, transportation, housing, and production of basic capital goods.

Social Characteristics

Together with economic considerations relating to lack of capital, many developing societies exhibit a number of common social traits that can only be touched upon here:

1. The relationship between the civil society and the state is highly unbalanced. In some countries, particularly in southern Mediterranean Europe, the state and its agencies overpower the civil society; the state plays a dominant role in providing services, jobs, and benefits. It is a far greater economic force than the state was in most liberal capitalistic economies of Western Europe. In contrast, the civil society is correspondingly weak and unorganized.

2. The middle classes, even with the advent of a commercial class and the beginning of industrialization, remain weak and unable to form the associations and representative parties and networks that shape and sustain the state. Liberalism and liberal capitalism and its political institutions, never having put down roots, are not valued.

3. In many of these societies, there is a latent or inherent tendency toward authoritarianism or statism; or, to put the same idea negatively, in many of them restraints against authoritarianism are few and weak. The state tends to incorporate rather than to represent interests; to formulate the public interest rather than to aggregate and synthesize it from among a number of conflicting demands and interests. Indeed, in all these societies interest articulation is generally weak. In most of them, it is the holders of coercive power, the military or the bureaucrats, who govern from above— through what Max Weber called "imperative coordination." Although it manifests itself in different ways, there is a latent authoritarianism in most of these societies.

4. When ruling bodies seek to mobilize and integrate local organizations and various interest groups, as they have since World War II, they do it from above. Integration and mobilization are pursued by a small elite through centrally controlled mechanisms—the single party, the bureaucracy, the army.

Economic Dependence or Independence

The relative degree of a nation's economic independence or dependence is a factor that directly affects the ideology and political direction in which socialist parties will move. It is a factor to which a great deal of attention has been paid. Countries of the Third World and Southern Europe share in varying degrees the characteristics resulting from dependency or semicolonialism. Some, especially in Southern Europe, entered the industrial-capitalist stage only after World War II. Despite a sizeable commercial class and significant developments in some industrial sectors they remain dependent for capital on the advanced economies of Western Europe, the United States, and, more recently, Japan. They produce most of the consumer goods they need but lag significantly in some, especially in durable consumer goods. Above all, their economies are characterized by heavy indebtedness and the lack of any real prospects of independent capital formation.

In all these societies, the imperative for industrialization and modernization is to find capital at home or to borrow it from abroad. In either case, tight political controls are required to hold domestic consumption down and to reduce welfare benefits and services. The imperative for industrialization calls for repressive legislation vis-à-vis trade unions and for the development of an ideology that emphasizes deferred consumption and the achievement of long-range national goals. Translated into political terms, such efforts lead to authoritarian regimes that have to pursue policies directly opposed to the pledges that socialist parties and movements had advanced originally.[4] There are, of course, some notable exceptions where oil provides the revenues for capital formation and investment, but the countries that have oil are few. Even among them, however, it will be some time before capital can be used for domestic investment in industry and in labor-saving technology.

The Appeals of Socialism

In the Third World and more recently in Southern Europe, the appeals of socialism as an ideology are many.[5] It conjures up many, often incompatible, visions of society. Foremost among these is social justice. Socialist ideologies project a conflictless, harmonious, and well-balanced society. They derive from an egalitarian ethic that rejects differences in status, wealth, property, and income and advocates an end to the privileges and rule of the few.

A second vision, not unrelated to social justice, is that of national integration and national independence. Socialism, by stressing communal integrative ties and extending them to the geographic areas where new nations have staked their claims, aims to provide for national unity and to promote the struggle for anticolonialism and political and economic independence. In many countries, socialism appeared as the corollary of nationalism and of national independence.

A third powerful vision that socialism has evoked almost everywhere in the Third World is that of rapid economic growth. It would provide the means and the incentives both to promote and telescope economic growth. Thanks to socialism, the new nations would achieve modernity without the social turmoil that capitalism caused in the West. Third World Socialists in essence advocated capitalism, but without the capitalist class and the proletariat and without the class conflict it had engendered elsewhere. Economic development was thus to be a process of economic growth and modernization without the methods used in the West after the Industrial Revolution. It would be cooperative, integrative, and planned rather than individualistic and conflictual, socially disruptive, haphazard, and chaotic. Thanks to socialism, the new nations would reconcile economic development with their indigenous cultural institutions and local tribal solidarities. (In Tanzania the term "Ujamaa" admirably combined nationalization, village socialism, and family subsistence economy.)

Thus socialism emerged as a doctrine and as a political movement destined to accomplish national independence from and against the West; modernization and rapid economic growth; social, national, and political integration; an end to class antagonisms and conflicts; and the realization of a modicum of social justice by providing for minimal material advantages at first and ever-expanding possibilities of well-being later on. The contradictions involved in the realization of these disparate aims, especially the requirement of modernization and economic growth on the one hand and welfare on the other, are quite apparent.

The Two Phases of Socialism

The contradiction between a mobilizing nationalist and welfarist ideology with the requirements of economic growth account for two forms or phases of socialism in the Third World. There is the millennial—a populist—phase of socialism followed by regime consolidation or regime maintenance. In the first phase, the pledges of social justice and the satisfaction of pent-up demands and expectations fuse with powerful national and social solidarity myths. The goal is usually to acquire power and gain or maintain support. The second phase corresponds to the hard realities of governance and managing with limited resources while trying to develop the prerequisites of national power—mostly a degree of economic sufficiency. The goal is to stay in power and to consolidate the newly established regime. For each phase, populism and regime consolidation, there are corresponding political forms of action, institutions, and ideologies.

Populism

Populism is fundamentally a protest movement that unites a disparate assortment of groups and classes for the realization of comprehensive and

PHASES OF SOCIALISM

	PHASE A — Populism	PHASE B — Regime Consolidation

Interests:	Farmers
	Workers
	Lower middle class
	Radical elites
	Marginals (urban villagers)
	Party rank and file
		Elites
		   Technocrats
		   Bureaucrats
		Industrialists
		   Financial and economic interests
		   Party leadership

Inputs:	Class and group demand Psychology (relative deprivation)	Capital formation Nascent industries Multinationals Banks
Structures:	Single party or single party dominance Party leader People's committees Front organizations Functions (mobilization and participation)	Bureaucracy State agencies Control agencies Police and army Party role waning (mobilization for support)
Ideology:	Nationalist Egalitarian Communalist Anti-elitist Participatory	Elitist Pragmatic Statist Authoritarian
Policies:	Welfarism Redistributive Consumer goods and services Protectionist	Save and invest Capital formation (capital goods) Durable consumer goods (if possible) Borrowing from international market

fundamental goals. It may come from the left or from the right. In the last thirty years or so, most Third World populist movements (but with notable exceptions, such as Iran) have combined socialism in the name of Marxism-Leninism with the inherited ideologies of the various countries in which they surfaced. Most but not all such populist movements have used the party as the instrument of mobilization and accession to power. Whatever its label, however, the party under these circumstances differs in structure and organization, membership and ideology, from other parties—whether democratic or Marxist-Leninist.

Populist movements have been particularly noticeable in societies that display the following characteristics usually related to social structure and economic development and their concomitant instabilities.

1. A fluid and changing class structure in which the peasantry begins to wane in favor of the working class. Populism attracts those who move from the village or country to the urban centers.
2. An unorganized working class and a weak middle class.
3. Low levels of political participation and of regime legitimacy.
4. A strong nationalist, independence, or irredentist movement.
5. An economy in a state of semicolonialism or dependency.
6. A surplus of intelligentsia, where surplus is defined in terms of function rather than numbers—that is, the availability of job opportunities within a system.

Populist ideologies tend to be messianic or personalistic. They promise heaven and they identify with the leader that promises to bring deliverance. They ignore the rational categories of causality and reject the historical categories of time—the phases and the steps needed to bring about the ultimate goals. As a result, they tend to emphasize will and power. Populist movements tend also to be integrative or communal. There is a Rousseauian element in all of them, a belief in the virtue and sovereignty of the collectivity. Finally, they profess to be egalitarian and put equality above individual freedom.

Populist movements are against the status quo and are a negation of the existing order. They profess to be anti-establishment and couch their ideology in negative terms: anti-class, anti-wealth, anti-foreign, anti-parliamentary, anti-individualist, anti-elitist. The typical populist ideologies consist of multiple negations that may find a common aggregation at a given time; they are ephemeral and ad hoc. Given the lack of a well-structured class system—indeed, given the fluidity of the class configuration—the alliances formed between various groups to sustain a populist movement are often based on incompatible perceptions of the interests involved, and as a result they are likely to break down. Populism is by its very nature, therefore, a transitory phenomenon.

There have been many cases of populism and populist movements in the United States, Canada, Western Europe, Latin America, and more recently in many of the new nations, so some generalizations about the major political characteristics of populism can be advanced.

First, populism has been a precursor of authoritarianism. It is a pre-fascist ideology.

Second, populist movements have appealed to the poor, the unemployed, the veterans, the lumpenproletariat, the farm hands, in general the marginals of all societies. Major strength and support has come from the small towns, from the countryside, the farm, and from among those who have little education. The middle classes do not at first lend their support. If and when they do, populism may become transformed into fascism.

Third, all populist movements have been strongly nationalistic and racist. They stress the integrity, independence, and purity of the nation. A national enemy from within or from without—real or imaginary—is singled out. There are always scapegoats in the populist ideology—the black, the white man, the Jew, the imperialists, the financial international conspiracy, the League of Nations or the United Nations, the Communists, the right or the left. In general, populism thrives when people are made to feel that there is a constant danger threatening them.

Fourth, many populist movements have borrowed heavily from the communist vocabulary and have adopted many communist techniques of political organization. In many new nations and semideveloped political societies, communism, Marxism, and populism often go hand in hand.

Fifth, populist movements have tried to organize a strong and well-disciplined party and to create numerous front organizations to permeate and control the whole society. While they have advocated direct power and control by the people, they have stressed the leadership of one man with ultimate authority to decide for all.

Finally, virtually all populist movements have appealed to the young. "Make room for us, you old ones" was one of the slogans of the Nazis in their early years.

In contrast to most political parties, populist movements (they make it a point of being "movements" and not "parties") have one common characteristic. They bring together all discontents into a vast protest movement. Populism, therefore, is above all a protest movement against past and present discontents and real or imaginary misfortunes. It is the sum total of many negations. Its role is to destroy, that by destroying it may pave the way to a new political and social order. But to do so, populism will have to transform itself. It may become authoritarian with the support of the middle classes, as was the case with the Nazis, the fascists, and the Peronists. Populism may also lead to a military dictatorship, as in many of the new nations and quite possibly in Iran. But it may also lead to authoritarianism from the left if and when there is a strong Marxist party.

Most Third World socialist movements have been populist movements at first. The party becomes the major vehicle of participation and mobilization, the symbol of national and social integration, and often the agency of governance. But above all, by expanding its base of support the party or movement increases the capabilities of the newly established government and promotes its legitimization.

Regime Consolidation

One-party socialism in many countries has given place to statist-bureaucratic socialism, or to military-bureaucratic socialism, or a combination of the two. The party eroded in favor of governance by a small political elite and its leader. This was true with Nasserism in Egypt and with the regimes in Iraq, Syria, and Tunisia. Even though the ruling party was never strong, this was also the case in Algeria. The changes from one-party rule to bureaucratic or military governance may be due to the major contradiction in Third World socialism, especially at its early stage, between populist ideology and the imperatives for regime maintenance through economic development and modernization.

After the acquisition of political power, the problem becomes one of consolidation. The emphasis shifts to performance. Change is geared to long-range goals of economic development. Ideology gradually stresses themes of social integration and symbols that elicit compliance. Ancillary institutional devices are developed to promote and implement compliance. Hard work, saving, and productivity are emphasized. In fact, the work ethic propounded is similar to the Protestant ethic. The new nations, particularly those that are relatively underdeveloped, begin to face the urgent need to build a new economy through investment in capital goods. This forces them to defer the satisfaction of consumer needs. The original electoral pledges of the populist phase have to be set aside, and this often necessitates the imposition of political controls. The populist phase and with it the mobilizing role of the political party, even if allowed to continue, is accompanied by selective methods and mechanisms of political constraint and even repression while ideology gradually shifts to rationalize the requirements of "law and order" and work.

More specifically, this regime-consolidation phase involves (1) an end to wage increases (indeed, a policy to reduce real wages), which often brings the regime in conflict with workers and trade unions; (2) a scaling down of welfare measures and welfare spending; (3) emphasis on capital formation and capital goods rather than consumer goods; and (4) a softening of intransigent ideological appeals in favor of an emphasis on specific needs such as procuring capital.

All such changes, in the name of economic development, have one major political consequence: an emphasis on authoritarian instruments of governance, often at the expense of the party.

The authoritarian model usually involves the following steps:

1. Upgrading the party leader and downgrading of party organs and front organizations through which support had been sought and mobilization and participation elicited. Party congresses and other representative bodies are neglected and eventually ignored.

2. Upgrading governmental structures, notably the bureaucracy. Populism gives place to statism. With statism the role of the expert and the technocrat grows.

3. Efforts by the government to control key associations, notably trade unions, farmer cooperatives, and professional associations, in order to silence the demands that such associations continue to represent.

4. Outright repressive tactics using the bureaucratic machinery and the police.

5. Ultimately, and as a last resort, the army emerges as an instrument of control and regime maintenance.[6]

Before we use this model to examine political trends and the evolution of the socialist movement in Greece, it may be worthwhile to point out the limits of its analytic utility. The model can help us only to identify certain broad trends that are colored by many indigenous cultural and social factors. Democratic socialism and Third World socialism—populist or statist—differ fundamentally from each other, however. The first accepts political pluralism and opposition; the second does not. The first represents and promotes the civil society and its various components, including the private economic sector. The second subordinates them to the party or the state and often to both. The transition from the populist phase, where the party plays a predominant role, to the statist phase, where the party becomes an auxiliary force, is not, however, clear. The single party and the state may vie with each other for dominance over a long period.

3 | Political Forces in Greece

On October 18, 1981, elections for the parliament (*Vouli*) were held in Greece. They resulted in a landslide victory for the left with the Socialists and Communists receiving almost 60 percent of the popular vote. It was the twelfth legislative election since World War II, a period during which Greece experienced a Civil War (1946–1949), a military dictatorship (1967–1974), and a change in regime from a constitutional monarchy (adopted on September 1, 1946) to a presidential republic (adopted on December 9, 1974).

After the Liberation in 1944 but more especially since 1950, rapid economic growth produced significant changes in the social structure of the country and altered dramatically the rural to urban population ratio. Today, less than 30 percent of the employed are farmers, and cities such as Athens, Salonica, and Patras have grown rapidly. More than 70 percent of the Greeks live today in urban centers of 100,000 and more. The country has become relatively prosperous, with per capita income rising to about $4,000 a year in 1981. There has been an expansion in manufacturing, in new industries, in food processing plants, and in chemicals and minerals to meet domestic needs and to provide exports for the Middle East. Employment increased rapidly, however, mostly in the tertiary sector—thanks to the expansion of tourism and related services.

The broad contours of Greece's international position remained the same until the 1970s. A member of NATO since 1951, Greece has been under the tutelage of the United States, on which it is dependent for military and economic aid. Turkey continues to be viewed as the traditional enemy, and the inability of Greece in 1974 to protect its ethnic brothers in Cyprus rankled the military and the elites, as did the growth of Turkish military power and U.S. support of Turkey. For the first time, the fate of the Greek islands in the Aegean and Greek sovereign rights over the Aegean Sea and the airspace above it appeared threatened. Détente, Greece's efforts to join the Common Market, and particularly the generally accepted proposition that NATO could not defend Greece against Turkey, another NATO member, accounted for a re-examination of Greece's position on the international scene.

Domestic socioeconomic changes and the changing international environment began to affect Greek politics. The military junta (1967–1974) attempted to freeze political changes and Greece's position. But after its downfall in 1974, these changes gathered momentum. The election of 1981 and the victory of PASOK, a self-styled Marxist socialist party, may well have been the culminating point of many of these changes.

Background

There are three major stages in the post–World War II political history of Greece, and party politics as well as electoral politics share common characteristics for each of them.

Counterrevolution and Restoration

The first stage began with the Battle of Athens in December 1944 and extended virtually until 1961. The first years were almost wholly devoted to dismantling the guerrilla government of the National Liberation Front (EAM), and to disbanding its fighting arm, the National Liberation Army (ELAS), both controlled by the communist party. It was a period in which the king returned; when foreign powers—England until 1947 and the United States thereafter—intervened in the most unqualified terms; when the notables and leaders of the political parties resumed control of the state machinery and rewove their web of influence and control based on family, local contacts, and personal favors; and during which the king and his entourage reasserted their personal prerogatives over the army and foreign policy. But it was also a period of rapid economic reconstruction, thanks to massive aid from the United States.

In accordance with the Truman Doctrine, the Atlantic Alliance, and NATO, the ideology that inspired and held together the political leadership was anticommunism. Its most overt manifestations were the outlawing of the communist party and the imposition of nationalist and civic orthodoxy on schools, universities, the civil service, newspapers, the judiciary, and most other state and social institutions.

Throughout this period the parties remained numerous and fragmented, forming coalitions and breaking them. They had few, if any, members and their quarrels were related to the division of spoils rather than to policy differences. The electoral system was constantly modified to suit particular interests and tactical considerations. In the first election after World War II, held in March 1945 under a simple proportional system, the so-called United Front of the National Minded (*ethnikofronon*) won a sweeping victory with 59 percent of the vote and an absolute majority in the *Vouli* (parliament). Another right-wing party under Napoleon Zervas (a former noncommunist guerrilla leader) won almost 7 percent of the vote. The centrist groups under such old-time liberal leaders as Sophocles Venizelos, George Papandreou, and Stylianos Sofoulis, won about 32 percent. The left was conspicuous by its absence. It boycotted the election. The election was held under the old registration rolls (last compiled in 1936) and it was alleged that a good percentage of those who voted had died, disappeared, or moved. The election was followed by the referendum on the monarchy in which almost 70 percent voted for the king's return.

Subsequent elections in this period showed the continuing fragmentation of political parties, the shuffling and reshuffling of various combinations of notables, and the personal character of ephemeral party labels. In 1950, for instance, eighteen parties participated and the same old-time leaders dominated the scene—Constantine Tsaldaris for the Populist Party, Venizelos for the Liberal Party, Nicholas Plastiras for a new coalition of various centrist political leaders, and Papandreou, whose party characteristically enough was labeled "Papandreou's Party" and received 14 percent of the vote. The four groups together received approximately 79 percent of the vote. A coalition of at least three of the four was needed to provide majority support for a government.

In the next election (1951), held under a reinforced proportional system, the right-wing groups under Gen. Alexander Papagos received 44 percent of the vote while the group headed by another general, Plastiras, managed 23.5 percent. The two generals had a majority in the *Vouli* but they could not agree. Yet their presence heralded the role of a politicized officer corps. The centrist groups received a little over 20 percent of the vote. For the first time since World War II the left was on the ballot but the United Democratic Left received only 7 percent of the vote.[1]

Given the nature of the party coalitions headed by the two generals, no discipline could be exerted on the deputies and a new election had to be held in 1952, this time, on the insistence of the U.S. ambassador, by a majority system. General Papagos won. He received 49.2 percent of the vote and 240 deputies out of a total of 300. But the center under Plastiras and Venizelos received 34.22 percent and the United Democratic Left improved its strength to almost 10 percent. The conservative forces strengthened their hold over the state and remained in control until 1956.

In brief, this first period was one in which a small oligarchy consisting of the army, the Crown, and the conservative political notables governed with U.S. support and economic aid. The forms of democracy were respected, but in substance the system was oligarchic.

The Opening

The second phase began with the legislative election of 1956 in which women voted for the first time. It was characterized by the restructuring of the party system, with two major parties vying for control. Some parties were led by newcomers as the old notables began to fade away. Constantine Karamanlis assembled the various fragments of the right—the Populist Party, the forces led by General Papagos, and some from among the Plastiras followers—to form a new party, the National Radical Union. It won 47.5 percent of the vote and 165 out of 300 seats. The centrists, on the other hand, and all the leftists joined forces in one formation, the Democratic Union, to win 48.2 percent of the vote, but under the electoral system they gained only 132 seats in the *Vouli*. Karamanlis and his party maintained their strength and their majority in the subsequent elections of 1958 and 1961, held under various electoral systems. The votes of the left and the center continued to represent almost half the electorate, however.

By 1961 party fragmentation seemed to give way to consolidation. The repressive legislation of the 1950s also began to be widely opposed. Anticommunism could no longer provide an adequate ideological front. The election of President John F. Kennedy in the United States ushered in a period of liberalization and after the Cuban missile crisis the Cold War gave place to an uncertain détente. With the rapid economic improvement and modernization, new groups and new interests began to press for internal reforms and liberalization. They challenged the role of the monarch and the influence of the Crown, and raised other issues as well.

The "opening" led to the electoral victory of George Papandreou in 1964 with 53 percent of the vote. The liberal center was now in a position to control the state, shape foreign policy, and subordinate the army. But it was pitted against the monarchy, which was supported by the military. The latter intervened in April 1967 to establish a military dictatorship that temporarily arrested this trend in the direction of liberalization.

Democracy at Last[2]

Historians who assess contemporary developments in Greece are inclined to give a great deal of weight to the military junta that ruled the country from

April 1967 until July 1974. The junta, born in secrecy, comprised no more than about fifty officers. It remained throughout its reign true to its origins. It did not form a party; it did not create new national myths and slogans; it did not aspire to a new political ideology or try to appeal to any given social class; it never attempted to mobilize the masses in favor of traditional or other values; it hardly even tampered with the basic Greek institutions—the village, the church, the business community, the upper bourgeoisie, or the army. It remained throughout its seven years of rule just as metallic and artificial as the insignia and the decorations of the officers in charge; it developed no popular roots. In the literal sense of the term it was a "band of gangsters." The manner in which it collapsed was itself an indication of its artificiality. The conspirators simply fell apart and asked the old political leaders to take over.

Having fallen, the junta became a nightmare that had been whisked away to allow a return to the status quo ante. The exiles came back; civil freedoms were restored; newspapers of all political colorations mushroomed; political prisoners were released; political parties and political leaders made their triumphant return to Athens. If the junta left any lasting effect, it was in the way in which the Greeks now looked upon the United States and its role. Through a curious but not unfamiliar process of displacement, the Greeks saw behind the ugly facade of the military dictatorship the United States and the Central Intelligence Agency. Inevitably, they put the blame on the United States. This perception only added to the artificial and foreign character of the military regime. Greeks referred to the seven years of the military dictatorship as the "occupation" (*katochi*)—a term specially reserved for the German occupation of the country during World War II.

With the fall of the junta in 1974, however, Greece continued to face the problems that had confronted the nation after World War II and again in the sixties, in fact, ever since it had gained its independence in 1827: how to move into a parliamentary democracy and translate Greek nationhood and independence into a stable political regime.

The Obstacles. To assess the return of democracy in Greece and its prospects, one must give an overview of the powerful forces that have impeded its growth and also point to some recent developments that may encourage it. Let us begin with the obstacles. The first has been the general sense of dependence of the Greek governing elites as well as of the public at large on the foreign powers that historically encouraged and nurtured Greek independence and on those that more recently have come to its aid and protection: England, France, Russia, and, after World War II, the United States. A second but related problem is the separation between the Greek elites and the people at large. A third, of more recent vintage, lies in the posture of the military and in their role after World War II. Each one of these forces relates to the others and accounts for a complex pattern of attitudes and behavior that defies an easy explanation.

"Dependence" is a term that may be conveniently used to cover such contemporary jargon as "semicolonialism," "neocolonialism," and "penetrated" systems. But dependence is a more accurate term, for it suggests an element that the others obscure: the overt complicity of the host country's elites with outside intervention and control, if not domination. Ever since Greek independence, this has been the role of the Greek elites. They solicited intervention; they relied on it and gradually took for granted the protection offered. A whole network of attitudes and expectations developed, leading to what amounted to institutional links with foreign powers. In the process, the attention of the Greek elites centered increasingly on their relationship with the protector. Through the Palace, and more frequently through the embassies of the foreign powers that dominated the scene, they made their demands known and received guidelines that set the course and determined the limits of their action. Major decisions were the result of the interplay between a foreign power and the Greek government, with the government's attitude ranging— depending on the circumstances—from abject submissiveness and obsequiousness to resentment and outright defiance.

It is important to recognize that a real game of politics for the highest stakes was played at this level. Occasional revolts against the dominant power were but the other side of the coin of dependence. For, gradually, as protection was taken for granted and aid was assumed to be forthcoming, any serious difficulty—domestic or, more often, international—was blamed on the protector. Thus the attitude of France and the indifference of England accounted, it was claimed, for the catastrophe of 1922 in Asia Minor and the victory of Turkey. More recently, it was the Kissinger tilt toward Turkey that allowed the Turks to invade Cyprus. While there may be elements of truth in both allegations, they do not tell the whole story. The Greeks and their government had their full share of responsibility.

The habit of dependence linked the Greek ruling groups with foreign powers and focused their attention on their relations with such powers to the detriment of developing solid popular roots and seeking popular support. Indeed, special historical reasons tended to make such a linkage between the people and their leaders more difficult in Greece than anywhere else. Modern Greece had been anointed in Elgin's marbles. The philhellenic movement was based on the "Glory That *Was* Greece," in an effort to rediscover and if possible resurrect it. After independence the ruling groups found it profitable to satisfy the expectations of the Western world. The language was purged to come as close as possible to ancient Greek. Literature and poetry at times reached comic levels of servile imitation of the classics. The church itself, even if unwilling to accept the pagan practices of antiquity, became the staunch defender of a language that was developed in the Hellenistic period. Culturally, linguistically, and politically, the line became sharply drawn between the elites and the people. As the character of the ruling groups changed, the distance between them and the people remained. The children of the wealthy and the educated invariably went abroad, to France and Germany, occasionally to England, and more recently, to the United States. They constituted a self-perpetuating group that drew its inspiration from the West and its support from among the foreign powers. The major institutions through which they expressed themselves were the palace, the bureaucracy, the universities, the army, and, depending on the internal political circumstances, the parliament.

Since political power came from abroad, the political elites did not attempt to secure it from within. This was the case even when, at the turn of the nineteenth century and the beginning of the twentieth, the country began to modernize, with growing urbanization, a network of communications, a national educational system, economic development, and the growth of a middle class primarily engaged in trade, manufacturing, and shipping. But modernization never led to the development of a broad consensus either on political goals or political means.

This lack of consensus became evident at three levels of political life. First the elites split, with some clustering behind the monarchy while others advocated social change and the establishment of genuine representative institutions. The conflict between modernizing elites, pleading for democratic institutions, and conservatives entrenched behind the Throne, became endemic. Second, even the modernizing elites were divided over the development of democratic institutions. Few went down the line in pushing for the formation of strong political parties, with mass membership, to act as transmission belts between the people and the government, to translate demands into policies, and mobilize and integrate the people into the system. Political demands and decisions were joined in terms of patron-client relations rather than a relationship between leaders and the rank and file. Parties became identified with powerful national leaders; Constantine Karamanlis and Andreas Papandreou are the living illustrations of personal politics. Generally, these leaders were local figures who formed loose coalitions and whose influence depended on the specific favors they could provide for their clients, who in turn would dispense favors to theirs, and so forth. Such a system can, of course, provide for a great degree of stability and even of consensus and effectiveness under certain conditions. But in a modernizing society patron-client relations are highly unstable. They shift constantly and the coalitions formed may either fail to respond to new demands or break up in the face of new demands. The parties therefore do not readily gain legitimacy and cannot provide an institutional apparatus strong enough to channel interests and provide for change. When the charismatic leader at the top falters or disappears, the party breaks up.

Hopeful signs. The real test of the viability and legitimization of democratic institutions came after the fall of the junta. In the 1974 election, the monarchy was set aside. The vote amounted to a reversal of the 1945 referendum, with two-thirds of the electorate now voting in favor of a presidential democracy and against the king's return (see Table 1). However, as under the Gaullist constitution, the president retains important personal discretionary prerogatives, including the right to call for a referendum. It is also noteworthy that since 1974 the electoral system has remained virtually the same—a reinforced proportional representation system. Thus the political parties were able to develop their electoral strategies and their organization and alliances within a stable framework of electoral rules and procedures. Finally, in 1974, the last installment on the mortgage of the Civil War was paid. The communist party, outlawed since 1946, was allowed to organize and run in the election.

Since 1974, genuine constitutionalism and liberalization have become the rule. Civil rights are fully guaranteed and protected; freedom of the press, speech, and association are staunchly upheld and elections are untainted by governmental intervention or fraud. The army, too, has come progressively under civilian control. Only small factions among the military and virtually none of the important political leaders advocate a change in the republican regime or a return of the monarchy. In short, there seems to be a legitimization of the regime or at least the formation of a broad consensus supporting it. The famous national schism, which pitted monarchists against democrats and

Table 1

RESULTS OF THE REFERENDUM ON THE MONARCHY
DECEMBER 8, 1974

Registered voters	6,244,539
Votes cast	4,719,787
Valid votes	4,690,986
Abstention rate	24.4%
Yes to king's return	1,445,875
	30.8%
No to king's return	3,245,111
	69.2%

SOURCE: General Secretariat for Press and Information, *Postwar Elections in Greece* (Athens: n.p., n.d.).

divided the parties, the army, and the elites, seems to have come to an end. But for how long remains a nagging question.

In 1981 the political system managed to accommodate not only party pluralism but also an increased polarization of the parties, with the left and the right confronting each other over a dying center. It was polarization, in Sartori's terms, that amounted to a confrontation.[3] Yet the system survived. The election of October 1981 involved fundamental choices about the economy, the society, political and institutional reforms, and foreign policy. That it took place in an orderly and peaceful way and that the transition to a self-professed Marxist and left-wing government, for the first time in the history of the country, was so smooth may be in itself the best indication of the legitimization of the regime.

Democracy and Elections Since 1974

The Election of 1974. Since 1974 there have been three legislative elections in Greece and one referendum on the king's return. While the latter was of crucial importance, the legislative elections of October 1974 and November 1977 maintained the dominance of the center-right groups and the leadership of Constantine Karamanlis. Very much like de Gaulle, he asked for and obtained solid majorities. His Nea Democratia party, which was formed in September 1974, managed to develop contacts rapidly throughout the country and was ready for the election less than ten weeks after the fall of the junta. But the other parties managed the same feat. This was another indication of the failure of the junta to seriously affect the existing political class. The Center Union, the newly founded PASOK led by Andreas Papandreou, and even the factions of the old communist party sprang into life. There were few independents and extremists from the left or the right, and they received less than 3 percent of the vote. The party system seemed to respond to the need for national identity and coherence, with only four parties running throughout the nation. The traditional fragmentation, provincialism, and even localism of the party system seemed to give way to broader national options presented by national, even if hastily organized, parties.

The Center Union, which had won a majority in 1964, was a ghost of its former self without a powerful personality to replace its former leader, George Papandreou. It continued to rely upon its traditional local and provincial leaders, but in the seven years of the junta many had abandoned their political strongholds or had failed to visit their constituencies. With Andreas Papandreou, the obvious heir to his father's position, the Center Union might have regained its vitality and appeal. But without him it stagnated. Besides, little that was substantive separated it from Karamanlis except its antiroyalist profession of faith. Even its strong pro-European stance, favoring entry into the Common Market and close relations with France, could not separate the Center Union from Karamanlis.

The left was represented by the Communists, who, if united, expected to receive the support of 10 percent of the faithful, and by PASOK, founded by Andreas Papandreou in the first week of September 1974. It was the latter that attracted popular attention.

Andreas Papandreou returned to Greece after seven years with personal aspirations that appeared to exceed his political grasp. He undoubtedly felt that the reaction against the junta would take a strong leftist and anti-American turn and expected to capitalize on this. In Portugal the pendulum had swung widely to the left; in Italy a leftist convulsion was averted only by the efforts of a vigilant communist party; in Spain the rumblings of an opening to the left could be heard. Papandreou opted for a new party; he chose to appear as a new man and he promised socialism overnight. He picked his targets carefully—NATO, Henry Kissinger, the Greek military, the multinationals, the American military presence in Greece, and, occasionally, Israel. He promised to secure for the first time the independence of Greece by cutting all ties with its protector, the United States, and also by eschewing any integrative ties with Western Europe and the Common Market. He watched vigilantly over the security and integrity of Cyprus, a member of the United Nations, hoping to keep the island out of any NATO entanglements and control. He urged the drastic purging of the Greek army and the setting aside of all legislation passed by the junta. But he went far to the left by advocating broad measures of socialization in industry, health, education, and even trade. He supported giving initiative and freedom of action to local regions and municipalities; granting equality of the sexes; guaranteeing the right to work; and, of course, he insisted on improving the quality of life. His platform combined parts of the French Common Program elaborated by the Communists and Socialists in 1972, invocations of the programs of left-wing extremists in Western Europe, and some of the realities of Swedish welfare legislation. It was much more to the left than what the Communists proposed, and the latter quickly accused Papandreou of adventurism and irresponsibility. The country, they claimed, was not ready for socialism. Not even the preconditions for socialism had been established, they contended.

With remarkable vigor, though he claimed to lack the financial means, Papandreou set out to organize his new party. Yet it was new only in part. Often he had to appeal to old-time centrists and to many local bosses who had worked with his father. He managed to set up local and provincial committees throughout the country and was able to stump the countryside, gathering large crowds at all his meetings. Students, intellectuals, and younger people flocked to his gatherings and some into his party, but the workers remained cool.

For a country that had just emerged from a military dictatorship, the election campaign of 1974 was a model of self-restraint and dignity. There was not a single instance of serious violence. The Greeks, in a remarkable fit of self-composure, decided to proclaim their pride in their newly found freedom and to show the world. It was perhaps the first genuinely free election the country had held since World War II. The results were also an expression of moderation, perhaps of conservatism. Greece simply failed to follow the example of Italy or Portugal, or even France. Karamanlis and his party swept the country with almost 55 percent of the vote, gaining 220 seats in the 300-member legislative assembly. He carried every single electoral district except Crete, the provincial bastion of the centrist party. Moreover, except for Crete, his nationwide vote was fairly evenly distributed: higher in the villages (about 58 percent), lower in the small and middle-sized towns (about 53–54 percent), and somewhat weaker in the large urban centers of Athens, Piraeus, and Salonica (where he scored about 49 percent).

The Center Union party, with about 20 percent of the vote, came second, but a very poor second at that, especially if we recall that some ten years before it had won an absolute majority of about 53 percent. It continued to rely on important local political magnates, but its leadership was gone and so was its appeal. There is no doubt that more than half of the centrist voters of 1964 and an appreciable part of the new voters went to the Karamanlis party, with a small fraction going to PASOK.

PASOK was the great unknown. It came in third with only 13.6 percent of the vote, gaining only 12 seats in the legislative assembly as compared to 60 for the centrists. This electoral defeat, however, tells only part of the story. Papandreou failed to get adequate support in the urban centers and among the workers. He dropped below his national average in large- and middle-sized towns and scored above it only in the villages and the countryside. In Athens and Salonica, for instance, he scored only 12.6 percent. There were some other disturbing signs in the PASOK vote. It was highly uneven, with wild ups and downs from one district to another, ranging from as high as 20–28 percent in some while dropping to 6–9 percent in others. The inference is inescapable: favorable party swings were often attributable to individual local candidates. The party seemed to attract a higher percentage of villagers than city dwellers and a greater percentage of voters from backward areas than from developed ones, and to owe its strength in specific areas to local candidates rather than to its program or leader. PASOK apparently benefited from the stagnation of the centrists rather than from the new urban political forces and the workers to whom Papandreou appealed.

This conclusion is borne out by the vote for the Communists. They held on to almost 10 percent of the vote, and their vote was distinctly urban. The Communists came out ahead of PASOK in Salonica, Athens, Piraeus, and other urban centers. Conversely, they simply wilted in the villages and more backward areas of the country. They won only eight seats in the legislative assembly. But after 35 years of repression and persecution (eased only in the early 1960s and then resumed with unmitigated vigor under the junta), the party—internally divided and without strong leadership—regained its strength.

The election, therefore, produced a solid parliamentary and popular majority. It also simplified the party configuration by narrowing competition to four parties. On the other hand, it did not provide a basis for the development of strong institutionalized national parties. Nea Democratia and PASOK were personal parties. As for the Center Union, it remained a loose alliance of local and provincial leaders. Nonetheless, the country could count at long last on a majority to undertake, even if with the utmost caution, the tasks ahead; drawing up a new constitution; gradually purging the army; achieving civilian control of the military forces; purging the civil service; negotiating with the United States regarding the American bases and NATO; settling the Greek-Turkish conflict; and implementing long overdue reforms in credit policy, taxation, education, labor legislation, urban renewal, and investments. What is more, after the election and despite anti-American sentiment, Greece remained solidly in the Western camp.

The Election of 1977. The election of November 20, 1977, almost exactly three years after the first post-junta election, virtually reproduced its basic left-right voter alignment. Nea Democratia, under the same leadership, won only a plurality and suffered a decline of 13 percentage points. In fact, however, about half of these defectors went to an extreme right-wing party, the National Alignment, which cooperated with Nea Democratia. The party's real loss, therefore, amounted to not more than 6 or 7 percentage points. If we add the votes of Nea Democratia, the National Alignment, and the Center Union, the total strength of the center-right in 1977 amounted to about 55 percent. On the left the most noticeable phenomena were the stability of the communist vote (around 10 percent) and PASOK's gains from 13.6 percent to 25.3 percent. Many of PASOK's votes came, therefore, directly from the center, but some may have also come directly from Nea Democratia. The combined vote of PASOK, the Communists, and the other leftists rose to about 35 percent from 25 percent in 1974.

Basically, the issues before the electorate in 1977 were the same as those in 1974. PASOK and the Communists refused to cooperate with each other, but they both harped on the same powerful nationalist slogans with regard to Turkey and Cyprus; they both exploited dissatisfaction with the United States and NATO; and they both argued strongly against Greece's entry into the Common Market. On economic and social issues, Papandreou continued to sound further left than the Communists, advocating structural reforms and a degree of socialization that the Communists were not yet ready to endorse. Nea Democratia stood on its record: prosperity, full employment, democracy, and political and social tranquility. The military had been brought under control. The European vocation of Greece, Nea Democratia claimed, was consistent both with the nation's traditions and with its future orientation. A cautious foreign policy had averted a confrontation with Turkey, and Greece had continued to maintain its distance from NATO. Karamanlis's personality and his ability to tame the generals and the colonels, to reorganize the armed forces, and to remain within the framework of the constitution and the political liberties it guaranteed assured his continuance as a national leader.[4]

When a new presidential election was held in April 1980, Karamanlis was the only candidate. The constitution requires that a presidential candidate obtain the votes of two-thirds of the 300-member *Vouli* to be elected. Failing this, the candidate must obtain a minimum of 180 votes in a second or third ballot; otherwise, a new legislative election is called. Karamanlis was elected with 183 votes on the third ballot. Nea Democratia, National Alignment, and some centrists voted for him. The other parties abstained. Thus, at the age of 73, the most popular leader assumed the highest office in the land. He pledged to be president of all the Greeks and to remain "above party."

4 | The Turn to the Left: The Election of 1981

Between 1974 and 1981, democracy functioned better than at any previous time in Greek history. Political and individual freedoms were protected, elections took place without accusations and counteraccusations of fraud, and critical decisions were made involving constitutional reform, the electoral system, important educational and social reforms, and, most important of all, the entry of Greece into the Common Market. Parliamentary institutions worked well. It was against this background that the third electoral contest took place—a contest that involved, as the Socialists continued to gain momentum, fundamental choices about the government, the economy, and the society.

It was an election that touched upon the redefinition of Greece's role and position in the world. To put it very simply, and by so doing to distort many complex issues, does Greece belong to the West, with which it is bound by innumerable intellectual and financial ties? Is it part of the Mediterranean world, linked with all the countries of the Mediterranean littoral? Is it Balkan, with geopolitical affinities and strategic interests binding it to the other Balkan nations? Or, finally, is Greece, given its rich and variegated past, a wholly distinct nation, robbed of its immense cultural treasures and heritage and bent upon redeeming its past?

To be sure, these questions were not raised before or during the election in this manner. But for the profoundly history-conscious Greeks they were implicit. For a long time, domestic Greek political cleavages related to foreign policy alignments—with France, England, Russia, and the United States. For a long time, too, two powerful forces, the Westernizers and the traditionalists, confronted each other. The first argued for rapid modernization, reforms, and political democracy and the second remained attached to traditional national and Christian values, to the preservation of the status quo and political paternalism—or, more recently, to authoritarianism. The division was compounded when issues of political and economic development were introduced: should Greece follow the Western model with Western attachments and Western help or should it follow one that obeyed its own special national and cultural imperatives? In the eyes of the left-wing parties, the West was now associated with capitalism and the multinationals and dominated by U.S. economic and strategic interests. The right-wing groups, on the other hand, had shifted their position to become increasingly pro-Western, expressing their attachment to the Common Market (after managing to engineer Greece's entry) and to NATO.

Both the army and the church—the pillars of traditionalism—wavered, as did the middle classes. After decades of subservience to Western and, more recently, American interests, the middle classes for the first time began to see their interests in terms of Greek attachments and identity. After 30 years of subordination to NATO and the United States, the army began to reconsider its national role in the face of the invasion of Cyprus and the Turkish threat to the Aegean. Ironically, it was the leader of the socialist party, Andreas Papandreou, a U.S.-trained economist, who upon his return espoused many of the traditionalists' themes while at the same time advocating the most comprehensive social, economic, and political reforms, many of them calculated to appeal to the enlightened segments of the middle classes and to the new managerial and technocratic elites. Papandreou became the champion of a new nationalism, skillfully blending the traditional loyalties of many Greeks with the Western and modernizing outlook of others. In so doing he seemed to transcend the old dichotomy between Westerners and traditionalists, to straddle the right and the left, and to appeal to both in the name of national independence. His stance against the Common Market and NATO appealed to the traditionalists, including the church and many in the army, but also to many businessmen, engineers, and technocrats, many of whom were, like Papandreou, trained in the West and anxious to assume control of their society's destiny. It also appealed to the left.

Another important issue that was implicit all along in the election was the legacy of the Resistance. The Greek resistance during the German occupation, widely sustained in a mood of resurgent nationalism, forged a vision of independence and social justice—very much as in Yugoslavia. Though led by the Communists, it was broadly supported by the people, especially in the countryside. The Resistance left a memory and a dream of a brighter, better, more equitable world—but a profoundly Greek world. Like all resistance movements it was intensely nationalist. The dream (a nightmare for others) remained, but the Battle of Athens and then the Civil War put an end to it. The excesses committed by the communist leadership alienated many of those who had been active.

It is very hard to determine exactly the role of the spirit of the Resistance in the election of 1981. But like the French socialist victory in that year, the Greek election and the victory of the Greek left echoed slogans from the past. The election was about Greek identity and Greek independence; PASOK's campaign had profound nationalist overtones. The left also made sweeping promises of social justice and equality in the name of socialism; it offered direct popular participation in decision making and the decentralization of authority to local bodies. PASOK rose against the establishment and appealed to all nonprivileged Greeks. It promised to purge the state and its adminis- trative agencies of those who had infiltrated them first under the shelter of the Germans and later under the protection of a foreign power, in order to end the "oligarchy" for good. PASOK proclaimed the imperative of an independent Greek strategy and foreign policy and glorified the Greek past. "Our glass is small but we shall drink from our glass," de Gaulle had said. For the Greeks it was "we shall be masters of our house."

The themes of social justice and national independence, of putting an end to the exploitation of man by man, revived the dream of the Resistance. For this reason, the election was highly ideological, if we use that term in its most comprehensive sense. Speaking a few days before the election, Papandreou promised that his generation would live up to the dream of the Resistance without making the mistakes its leaders had made 40 years earlier. (He did not specify the mistakes.) This intensely nationalist and ideologic element is one of the intangibles of the 1981 election. It cannot be easily documented or quantified but may explain, at least in part, why the middle classes rallied behind PASOK.

Two major traits have characterized the Greek middle classes: (1) their inability to guarantee Greek independence—accepting and often soliciting foreign tutelage and protection; and (2) their failure to establish viable demo- cratic institutions, whether under a hereditary monarch as in England, Hol- land, and the Scandinavian countries or under a presidential system, as in France. All along, the middle classes have been uneasy about their Greek identity, unwilling to become a part of the country to which they belong, planting no roots, roaming far and wide in Europe and elsewhere. Greece was much more an idea than a reality. Similarly, the economic interests of the Greek middle class were identified with the interests of the European indus- trial and commercial groups whose agents in effect they became. It was compradore capitalism.

Uncertain about their own identity, drawing a sharp distinction between their class and the common people, unwilling or unable to make democracy work and to provide the proper reforms in education and the government so that the people could begin to actively participate, the middle classes in time of crisis invariably switched to right-wing antidemocratic solutions. The years of Elefthezios Venizelos were followed by John Metaxas and Queen Frederika. British protection was replaced by the American version. Whatever glimmer of hope there might have been that a reconciliation could take place between the people and the middle class after the liberation of Greece in 1944 vanished. Would Papandreou and his socialist movement manage some 40 years later to bring the Greek bourgeoisie back into the nation by soliciting and getting their participation and support? It was, and remains, a crucial question.

Electoral Issues and Platforms

The Panhellenic Socialist Movement continued to reflect many disparate background forces and to raise them to the level of political consciousness.[1] The movement echoed many of the slogans of the Resistance. It was strongly nationalist; it asserted Greece's need for an independent posture in foreign policy and strategy; it appealed to and mobilized both the beneficiaries and the victims of economic modernization—both the new modernizing managerial elites and the villagers, artisans, and farmers who had moved into urban poverty and to whom, in the name of socialism, PASOK promised a better world. It pointed an accusing finger at the establishment's failure to achieve reforms in education, housing, and social services, an establishment that had grown increasingly complacent to the point of indifference. Finally, PASOK promised to liberate Greece from the tutelage of the monopolies and the multinationals and to draft development goals consistent with the needs of the Greek economy and society.

What were the major issues before the electorate? First, national independence. Papandreou remained hostile to the Atlantic Alliance and NATO and promised to hold a referendum on Greece's membership in the Common Market. The defense of Greece should be Greek, he had asserted many times, having in mind the Turkish threat. But he also wanted to challenge Turkey's occupation of 38 percent of Cyprus's territory and to protect the ethnic Greeks there. On negotiations with Turkey, Papandreou's position remained intransigent—there was nothing to negotiate. He insisted that all matters regarding the continental shelf, the Aegean airspace, and the territorial sovereignty of the Greek island over the sea coast were governed by existing treaties.

The time had come, so Papandreou asserted, for full Greek independence in domestic affairs and in foreign policy. This call for independence was to signify a clean break with the past. The election, therefore, appeared to many an opportunity, as never before, to assert their Greek national identity—

almost to rediscover it. It was a call for independence addressed against Turkey, the United States, Europe, and the Common Market.

The second component of the platform was socialism; PASOK claimed to be a Marxist party, committed to the socialization of the economy. While details were never clearly spelled out, the party clearly envisioned nationalization of parts of trade, industry, and mineral wealth. Such a program would normally frighten many among the middle and lower middle classes in Greece. But a fresh and powerful breeze filled Papandreou's sail when François Mitterrand and the Socialists won in France in June 1981, just four months before the Greek election. France remains the home of most of the Greek intelligentsia. Papandreou himself was quick to exploit the socialist victory in France, and to present himself as a "Mitterrand Socialist," clearly giving the impression that PASOK would follow the model of Western socialism.

PASOK insisted on its attachment to democracy, but with two important reforms. One was decentralization of the state apparatus, again a measure calculated to satisfy the voters outside of Athens. The other was *laokratia*, which literally means direct popular government. Decentralization and *laokratia* together amount to direct self-government not only at the local, municipal, and regional levels, but also in the firm, the factory, and the various public establishments. Since one of Papandreou's socialist goals was the establishment of cooperatives among the farmers, self-government could be extended to them, too.

Only matters of emphasis separated the Communist Party of Greece (KKE) from PASOK. The KKE appeared more radical in matters of foreign policy, asking for the immediate, definitive, and complete withdrawal of Greece from NATO, the withdrawal of U.S. forces from Greece, the closing of all U.S. bases, and the withdrawal of Greece from the Common Market, so that "the national interests of Greece would not serve imperialism." It demanded the removal of nuclear weapons from Greek territory and endorsed Leonid Brezhnev's proposal for a treaty between Greece and the Soviet Union that would exclude the use of nuclear weapons in the event of war. With regard to the economy, on the other hand, the KKE appeared more moderate than PASOK. "Patriots," the platform statement began. It called for the democratization of publicly owned and controlled enterprises and the extension of socialization to energy and all enterprises of national import. The rest of the platform covered familiar ground, including decentralization, popular participation in the economy and the administration, larger retirement pensions, public housing, and free and expanded education. The KKE also called for the introduction of a simple proportional representation system and constitutional reform to eliminate the special and personal powers granted to the president of the republic.

Nea Democratia ran on the platform of "Renewal" (*Ananeossis*).[2] Without their popular and charismatic leader, Constantine Karamanlis, who had been elected president of the republic, and plagued with dissension among its top leaders, Nea Democratia continued in substance as a party of notables and bosses. Despite many efforts, it had failed to develop an organization. It stood on its record. In their seven years in office the party's leadership had scrupulously maintained constitutional liberties, kept Greece to the lowest unemployment rate in Europe, promoted modernization of the economy (Greek per capita income rose to equal Spain's and to compare favorably with Italy's) and brought Greece into the Economic European Community as a full member. Inflation marred the record, averaging 22–23 percent a year, and turned out to be one of the crucial issues in the eyes of the electorate. Urban living conditions and services, notably in the Athens region, had deteriorated and pollution had become endemic. Educational facilities continued to be inadequate, despite the establishment of provincial university centers. The Civil Service remained bloated and inefficient. Above all, corruption remained unchecked. Nea Democratia continued to distribute favors and subsidies to friends and supporters. After seven years in office, it was faced with a backlog of unsolved problems and mounting grievances.

The Results: A Macroanalysis

The election of October 18, 1981, resulted in an unprecedented victory of the Greek left. The pro-Soviet communist party (Kommunistikon Komma Ellados; KKE) won 10.9 percent of the vote while the Eurocommunist party (Kommunistikon Komma Ellados-Esoterikou [Interior]; KKE-I) received a mere 1.4 percent. PASOK (Panellenio Sosialistiko Kinima) won 48 percent of the vote. Thus the combined left received 60 percent of the total vote cast (see Table 2).

Equally unprecedented was the collapse of the center. Ever since 1946, the center had managed to receive from 20 to 53 percent of the vote, whether running under different labels, united, or divided. In the election before the junta takeover in 1964, the Center Union, under the leadership of the late George Papandreou, had received 53 percent of the vote. In the election of 1974 the Center Union, without George Papandreou, won over 20 percent. In 1977 it dropped to about 12 percent, the first clear indication of decline. In 1981 the combined vote of the various centrist factions totaled only 3.5 percent.

The so-called right came out badly mauled. In 1974 Nea Democratia received 54.37 percent of the vote; in 1977 Nea Democratia and a rightist group, the National Alignment, received 41.84 and 6.82 percent, respectively, for a total of 48.66 percent. In the election of 1981 Nea Democratia,

Table 2

ELECTION RETURNS

	1974		1977		1981	
	Votes	Seats	Votes	Seats	Votes	Seats
Nea Democratia	2,669,133 (54.37%)	219 (73%)	2,146,365 (41.84%)	171 (57%)	2,033,584 (35.86%)	115 (38.3%)
National Front	–	–	349,988 (6.82%)	5 (1.7%)	–	–
Center Union Party	1,002,559 (20.42%)	60 (20%)	612,786 (11.95%)	16 (5.3%)	23,723 (0.42%)	–
Various centrists	–	–	55,498 (1.08%)	2 (0.7%)	207,464 (3.20%)	–
PASOK	666,413 (13.58%)	13 (4.3%)	1,300,025 (25.34%)	93 (31%)	2,725,132 (48.06%)	172 (57.3%)
United Left (including KKE and KKE-I)	464,787 (9.47%)	8 (2.7%)	–	–	–	–
KKE	–	–	480,272 (9.36%)	11 (3.6%)	619,292 (10.92%)	13 (4.3%)
KKE-I	–	–	139,356 (2.72%)	2 (0.7%)	77,461 (1.37%)	–
Total ballots cast	4,908,974*		5,129,177*		5,636,436*	

*Includes invalid ballots not counted in party vote returns.

SOURCES: Greece, Ministry of the Interior, Election Directorate, *Apotelesmata ton Vouleftikon Eklogon tis 17ts Noemvriou 1974* (Results of the parliamentary elections of November 17, 1974), vol. 1 (Athens: National Printing Office, 1976); idem, *Apotelesmata ton Vouleftikon Eklogon tis 20is Noemvriou 1977* (Results of the parliamentary elections of November 20, 1977), vol. 1 (Athens: National Printing Office, 1979); and *General Elections, 18 October 1981, for the Greek Parliament* (Athens: General Secretariat for Press and Information, 1981).

with which the National Alignment had merged, received 36 percent of the vote, a loss of almost 13 percent (see Table 2).

The Swing

Between 1977 and 1981 the swing from the center-right to the left amounted to about 25 percent—and virtually all of it went to PASOK. With about 5.6 million voters (there were about a half million new voters), at least 1.3 million who had voted in 1977 either for the Center Union, Nea Democratia, or the National Alignment shifted their votes to PASOK. More than half of the voters who shifted (at least 600,000) came from Nea Democratia and the National Alignment. Nea Democratia went progressively down; the Center Union's decline was consummated; the left—especially PASOK—gained rapidly in almost arithmetic progression, rising from 13.6 percent in 1974 to 25 percent in 1977 and 48 percent in 1981.

Swings are common phenomena to those familiar with Greek politics. Indeed, ever since 1946 there have been many shifts from one party to another. Yet the differences in 1981 are significant. First, the same party labels in past elections covered changing coalitions of powerful political leaders and bosses, so the swing was often predictable and attributable to the current electoral alignments among the leaders. Second, the genuineness of a swing was always in doubt, since elections were often manipulated. Third, constant changes in the electoral law had an unavoidable impact upon the parties and the voters. Fourth, foreign pressure had a special weight with the voters, the parties, and the government holding the election. In the election of 1981, the swing represented the continuation of a trend that began in 1974 with virtually the same party configuration and the same electoral system. All elections since 1974 have been held under conditions of perfect freedom and without any visible outside influence or pressure, to say nothing about fraud or intervention.

The Electoral System

The electoral system in 1981 remained the same as in 1974 and 1977. The total population was divided by the number of parliamentary seats to be filled (288 of the 300) to arrive at the apportionment of seats for each of the 56 electoral districts. (The twelve remaining seats, for "state deputies," were apportioned later to the political parties that received 17 percent or more of the vote, on the basis of their nationwide electoral strength.) The only difference in 1981 was that the political parties were allowed to nominate one, two, or three candidates more than the number of seats apportioned for each electoral district. Under this system, the electoral quotient needed to win a seat is arrived at by dividing the total number of votes cast in each district by the number of seats allotted to it plus one. Thus in an electoral district that is allotted three seats and in which 100,000 people vote, the quotient is 25,000. Parties that receive 25,000 votes or more are entitled to a seat. Voters are allowed to mark their preferences for a given candidate on the party list by putting a cross before his name.

After the first distribution of seats, the remainders are added up within larger electoral districts composed of a number of the original ones within designated geographic areas and the same operation is repeated. The additional remainders are then added up and allotted in a third and last distribution. With 56 electoral districts, the number of voters in each varies and the quotient varies accordingly. In some districts, seven or eight thousand voters may elect one deputy; in others, notably in the big urban centers, it may take double this number.

Despite its proportionality, the system continues to favor the large parties in at least two ways. Parties that receive less than 17 percent of the national vote cannot participate in the second and third distributions; they lose all their remainders. Also, they cannot share in the election of the twelve state deputies.

In the previous two elections, the electoral system had favored Nea Democratia; in 1981 it favored PASOK, which with 48 percent of the total vote elected 172 deputies, or 57.3 percent of the *Vouli*. The system also led to the elimination from the *Vouli* of all parties other than PASOK, Nea Democratia, and the communist party. But in 1981 the KKE failed to get 17 percent of the vote and did not participate in the second and third distributions; therefore it had no share of the twelve state deputies. With a little over 10 percent of the vote it received less than 5 percent of the seats in the *Vouli*. Under a straight system of proportional representation (PR), which had been advocated by PASOK and KKE, the distribution of seats would have been as follows: Nea Democratia, 108; PASOK, 144; KKE, 33; centrists, 9; KKE-I, 3; others, 3. A PR system, in other words, would have deprived PASOK of an absolute majority of the seats and would have forced it to seek some kind of cooperation with the communists or the centrists.

Voting Patterns

What is of particular interest is the national distribution of the PASOK vote. It fell below 40 percent in only 7 of the 56 electoral districts. Variations between the urban and rural vote were insignificant, dispelling the early assumption that PASOK was primarily an agrarian party. In fact, it received a slightly higher percentage of votes in the urban centers than in the countryside. In many districts, unless a powerful centrist political leader had joined Nea Democratia, PASOK gained the overwhelming majority of centrist voters.

There is no indication whatsoever that any communist votes went to PASOK, as they did to Mitterrand on the first ballot of the French presidential election and on the first ballot of the legislative election that followed. On the contrary, the Communists increased their strength, an increase that came in part from new voters or from former PASOK voters. The spectacular swing in the direction of PASOK came exclusively from the center and the right.

A comparison of the results of 1974 and 1977 with the results of 1981 indicates two mutually reinforcing trends. First, in all the districts where the Center Union had scored above its national average in the previous two elections, PASOK did better in 1981 than its own national average; it absorbed the centrist strongholds almost everywhere. In some regions—Crete for instance—where the liberal-centrist vote had been traditionally strong, PASOK also exceeded its average. The swing from Nea Democratia to PASOK between 1977 and 1981 appears on the other hand quite uniform and amounted to at least 30 percent of Nea Democratia and National Alignment voters. They and the overwhelming majority of centrist voters, as well as a good percentage of new voters, boosted the total PASOK vote from 1.3 million in 1977 to 2.7 million in 1981. The communist left gained only a little —the transfer was made from the right and the center to PASOK. This distinguishes sharply the Greek from the French election, where transfers toward the socialist party were made both from the communist left and from the center.

While it is important to note the source of PASOK's new votes, it is equally significant to know where Nea Democratia lost its voters. The answer is relatively simple and carries with it a message for the future. Primarily, the urban voters who had voted for Nea Democratia in 1974 and 1977 moved to PASOK. Conversely, in most of the countryside a smaller percentage moved to PASOK, although local factors account for variations. As for new voters, they went overwhelmingly to PASOK and KKE.

If we recall that some 31 percent of the voters in 1974 voted for the return of the monarchy and if we compare the distribution of votes for the monarchy in 1974 with the distribution of votes for Nea Democratia in 1981, we find a striking similarity. Nea Democratia had shrunk to a hard core of pro-royalist and even right-wing forces so that the refashioning of a reformist Right in Greece—initiated under Karamanlis and continued on into the 1970s—may be difficult.

The KKE failed to gain significantly from the left-wing trend. It even fell short of its strength in some previous elections in which the Communists had collaborated covertly with various leftist formations under different labels. For instance, in 1958 the United Democratic Left won almost 25 percent of the votes. In the election of 1963, they won 14.34 percent. In 1981 PASOK appeared as a dam holding the communist left at bay. It did not penetrate any communist strongholds as the Socialists did in France but simply prevented them from flooding new territories.

While the victory of PASOK was unprecedented for a self-professed Marxist party, the composition of its electorate raises disturbing questions for its future. Before the emergence of PASOK, the centrist parties (with or without the support of the left) had done as well or even better than PASOK's score in 1981. In 1956 the Democratic Union received 48.15 percent of the vote. In 1951 centrist groups managed better than 53 percent. In the last election before the military junta in February 1964, George Papandreou's Center Union received almost 53 percent of the vote. Despite their spectacular victory, Andreas Papandreou and PASOK, while keeping the Communists at bay and making deep inroads into the centrist and conservative vote, did not do as well as his father and the Center Union Party did in 1964 and as undoubtedly he would have done had an election been held in May 1967.

The election results, on the other hand, set the parameters within which PASOK can operate electorally. It cannot improve its strength but it can lose it fast. There is no electoral space to its left into which it can move. On the contrary, the Communists will continue to appeal to the PASOK militants and ideologues and remind the voters of all the many campaign commitments that PASOK may not be able or may not wish to keep. PASOK cannot make any further inroads into the center or the conservative electorate. Both centrists and conservatives who voted for PASOK will cling to their hopes and expectations, not the least of which are the material rewards that control of the state always provides to those who have given their support to the government; and they will resent failure and omissions. In the near future, especially as the new election approaches, the electoral strains on PASOK may become as severe as its victory was great.

5 | 1981: A Critical Election or a Protest Vote?

My purpose here is to dwell on major electoral trends and discuss retrospectively and prospectively the evolution of Greek politics in the light of the election of 1981. Was that election indicative of major political and structural changes? Can it be considered a critical election, denoting major shifts in group alliances, alignments, and supports, or was it indicative and characteristic of a vast protest movement behind a leader who knew how to exploit all its various—and often contradictory—elements? In the latter case, the overwhelming victory of PASOK may be only episodic.

A critical election, Dean Burnham wrote, is one in which a radical realignment of support occurs both within and from one to the other of the major constituency parties.

> Eras of critical realignment are marked by short, sharp reorganizations of the mass coalitional bases of the major parties which occur at periodic intervals on the national level; are often preceded by third party revolts which reveal the incapacity of "politics as usual" to integrate, much less aggregate, emergent political demand; are closely associated with abnormal stress in the socio-economic system; are marked by ideological polarizations and issue-distances between the major parties which are exceptionally large by normal standards; and have durable consequences as constituent acts which determine the outer boundaries of policy.[1]

Burnham was quick to point out that his definition would not necessarily fit the class or ideological parties of Europe. But I do believe—and an examination of the Greek parties since 1946 bears me out—it could apply to the Greek parties. They have been constituency parties, umbrella organizations held together through regional and local alliances and agreements among local bosses with an eye to spoils. They have been representative of temporary and shifting alliances of major socioeconomic and political interests and of major organizations, including farmers, small businessmen and manufacturers, shipowners, banking and foreign capital, tobacco growers, the bureaucracy, the army, the church, the Crown, and occasionally even the ambassadors of the major European and more recently some non-European powers.

A protest election, or rather a protest vote, is symptomatic of general and widespread dissatisfaction with a given government, its leaders, and its policy. But more often, protest and a protest vote involve much more and are addressed to the fundamental issues of the polity, the society, the economy, and the nation. A protest vote in a given election may relate to problems of access, the entry of disfranchised groups into the political process; to the equitable distribution of resources for those who consider their share inadequate; to the redress of a national misfortune; or to other major policy questions. A protest vote often stems from profound psychological causes—the search for status, the defense of status when it is endangered, or racial or ethnic affirmations. It becomes a way for the insecure and the alienated to express their fears and anxieties. It is often the manifestation of pent-up demands and aspirations. A protest vote in an election is often associated with the appearance of a new (or third) party and a new political leader. In this sense, most protest votes amount to considerable swings away from the established parties. They are harbingers of a critical election, but one must wait for future elections to be able to tell. A protest vote, in other words, may or may not have the "durable consequences" that a critical election produces.

The criteria I suggest to distinguish a protest vote from a critical election lie in the stability, structure, and coherence of the realignments. By "stability," I mean the prospects of continuation; by "structure," the realignment of voters in terms of group affiliations and attachments rather than in terms of individual affiliation and preferences. By "coherence," I mean the compatibility on policy issues of the groups that shift. Naturally, if a number of social and other groups shift position in an election, the ultimate question to ask is: How likely are these groups to remain together? No empirical test can help us answer this question until some time has passed, usually until subsequent elections take place. For instance, it was not until 1936 that one could say in retrospect that the election of 1932 in the United States was critical. But we can rephrase the question and ask: How congruent are the shifts, or realignments, of various social groups with regard to both political ideology and policy objectives in any given election? In short, is there agreement and compatibility among them or are the shifts attributable to different and often contradictory perceptions and policy expectations? If there is agreement and compatibility, then one can tentatively say that an election such as the 1981 Greek election was critical indeed and may have durable consequences. If the shift is attributable to different and contradictory perceptions and policy expectations, then a strong argument could be made that it was a protest vote and unlikely to be repeated.

A Critical Election?

Some will argue that the election of 1981 even though, or perhaps because, it was the culmination of trends that began in 1974 and before, was a critical election. It broke the stable coalition of political supports and alliances that existed between 1946 and 1967 and produced new ones.

The Stable Synthesis

What were the major elements of the existing stable synthesis? First, cooperation among the middle classes and the traditionalist forces: the peasantry, the church, the army, and the Crown. To be sure, there were conflicts and frictions between and among them but the major ones related to the distribution of favors and spoils. These groups were bound together by a common fear of the left, while excluding by and large the workers (on the left) and the peasantry from genuine political participation. The democracy that existed after the Liberation had all of the characteristics of an oligarchy.

There was stability in the existing political practices and political parties, what might be called the modus operandi of the system. It relied on patron-client relationships, favoritism in the bureaucracy, and concessions to powerful economic interests, including foreign companies and multinationals. The system also accepted implicitly the role of the monarch in some of the commanding centers of decision making, such as defense and foreign policy. Even George Papandreou did not challenge such personal prerogatives. But like Venizelos half a century before, he simply felt that after an election the king should yield to his prime minister and allow him to appoint his own cabinet members, including the minister of defense. But the king continued to manipulate the members of parliament and managed to split Papandreou's party.

The modus operandi of the political parties and their organizations was also widely accepted: they remained parties of notables, based on regional and local coalitions, with little organization and discipline and without mass membership. It was a situation that made shifts and changes based on personal, family, and local considerations easy.

There seemed also to be a stable consensus with regard to the constitution and major political institutions. Both center and right accepted administrative centralization and an inflated bureaucracy and often used the latter as an instrument for rewarding supporters. The role of the monarch was accepted, even if grudgingly by some. Significantly enough, the first opening with regard to the monarchy was made by the military junta in December 1967; or rather, it came about because after a conflict between the king and junta the king was forced to leave. The military junta also was indirectly responsible for undermining the position of the oligarchy by imposing a repressive authoritarian system that threatened the existing elites and the oligarchy itself. When the dictatorship collapsed, many of the elites who had suffered at its hands became overtly hostile to military regimes.

There was also widespread agreement on the economic system that prevailed. Free enterprise was accepted; foreign investments were welcomed; free trade was extolled; emigration abroad was encouraged; and the service nature of the economy—an outgrowth of tourism—was supported. It was only after 1974 that genuine welfare legislation was seriously undertaken.

A common ideology—or rather, a common lack of ideology that we might call pragmatism—united the oligarchy both at the center and the right. Under the aegis of the patron-state, the United States, the oligarchy shaped economic policy, social policy, and above all, foreign policy in accordance with the constraints imposed and the opportunities offered by the international environment. One departure from pragmatism was the intense anticommunism shared by all the members of the oligarchy. It helped reinforce Greece's position in NATO and was used to exclude many workers, peasants and university students from political participation. Anticommunism bolstered authoritarianism in the civil service, the police, the army, the university, and the church.

These were, briefly, the elements of the stable synthesis that had been fashioned. It was centralizing, oligarchic, authoritarian. Yet a number of destablizing forces were already apparent that foreshadowed the rapid evolution of political forces after the fall of the military dictatorship in 1974 and may have accounted for the results of the election of 1981.

Destabilizing Forces

The weight and relevance of some of the destabilizing forces can be easily discerned after 1974. There was the discrediting of the military, both because of the primitiveness and brutality of its regime and because of the incompetence and paralysis it showed in the face of the Turkish coup-de-main in Cyprus. The army became separated from the other elites, a separation that broke a strong link in the chain that had held them all together.

The second destabilizing force was the disappearance of the monarch, another powerful link. There were also profound changes in the socio-economic structure and their attendant psychological and political manifestations—in a word, modernization. The rapid exodus from the farm to the towns began to have a cumulative impact in the early 1970s; more than 1.5 million in a population of 9 million moved from the countryside to urban centers. They constituted a group that was a mix of lumpenpeasantry, lumpenproletariat, and lumpen–petit bourgeois, sharing the expectations of city dwellers without the amenities of city life, drawn increasingly into the tertiary sector of employment or becoming artisans and small shopkeepers while maintaining all along their peasant attachments. Even if sheltered by the multiple networks of family relations, most displayed all the characteristics of the uprooted— nostalgia for the past and for their village, yet searching for a new life and for cooperative and associational activities that did not exist. It was, and remains, a powerful and volatile group.

Another powerful destabilizing force was the rapid economic growth of the 1950s and 1960s. Through full employment it provided a minimum degree of shelter and satisfaction that met the demands of many but also whetted their appetite for more. As long as a balance, relatively speaking, could be kept between wants and demands on the one hand and fulfillment and satisfaction on the other, the oligarchy and the stable synthesis they had fashioned were safe. But after 1974 it became increasingly difficult to keep that balance. Wants and expectations in health, education, entertainment, leisure, urban transportation, housing, and retirement benefits began to exceed available resources—or rather, the resources that the oligarchy was willing to provide. Relative deprivation was the experience of many.

The challenge could have been met, if the oligarchy had managed to close ranks. But with the monarch in exile, the army discredited, and many of the political elites, including the leaders of Nea Democratia, completely disenchanted with the military, the oligarchy broke apart. The defection of the middle classes and the search for a liberal synthesis in politics, a reformist policy in the economy, and a revisionist policy in foreign affairs provided the foundations for a new political ideology.

The political modus operandi also began to change after 1974. The political party appeared increasingly as a vehicle for political participation. The parties became fewer in number and better organized; they began to search for and acquire a mass membership and following. Demands were made for the organization of a rationalized bureaucracy to mete out services and benefits on the basis of impersonal and objective criteria. Nepotism began to give place to group considerations, and favoritism to recruitment based on talent and merit. Authoritarian and elitist practices in the universities, the police, the bureaucracy, and the army became more difficult to shelter from public scrutiny and criticism.

Finally, détente broke another link in the stable synthesis on which the oligarchy rested. It made anticommunism obsolete. It also put Greece's foreign policy and strategic position into a different perspective. Prior to the election of 1981, the leaders of both PASOK and Nea Democratia seemed to agree that there was no danger to Greece from the north, thus muting many arguments favoring Greece's membership in NATO. And while anticommunism was becoming obsolete, a new, intense and profoundly unifying theme reappeared on the eastern horizon, namely, Turkey. The Turkish threat triggered all the traditional nationalist reflexes and provided PASOK with its most powerful ideological slogans and electoral support.

To a public intensely disenchanted with the Turkish occupation of a significant part of Cyprus and with the inability or unwillingness of the United States to enforce an acceptable solution, nationalism quickly became translated into anti-Americanism and even anti-Europeanism.

The elite groups, united thus far, split on almost all these revisionist options. Many of the traditionalists were deeply attracted by nationalism but so were the middle classes, though the latter remained wary of forcing the issues of NATO and the Common Market. Others saw an opportunity in the name of both nationalism and socialism to assume political power and with it the control of their country's destiny. Thus the unity of the oligarchy was destroyed. Between 1974 and 1981, there was more movement and less order in Greek politics than ever before since 1945.

A New Realignment?

It can be argued that 1981 was, therefore, a critical election. It afforded an opportunity for a shift of allegiance to PASOK by sizeable segments of the voting population that had supported the oligarchy, neutralized others, and, more importantly, provided a vehicle of political access to the new groups and gave them a chance to assume political power. Even if PASOK proves to be a third party, its victory may ultimately infuse the Center Union Party with new ideas and policies and new supports. Otherwise, the victory of PASOK may amount to a massive realignment of the centrists and some of the traditional elements behind it. It only failed to get the vote of the workers in the urban centers that went to the KKE. The realignment of forces brought about the isolation of the conservative groups and reduced support for Nea Democratia to the monarchists, some hard-core conservatives, and assorted right-wingers, many of whom remain nostalgic for authoritarian solutions.

The victory of PASOK may also bring about a radical change in the political modus operandi continuing the trends already noted. PASOK is a national party, a mass party, and a highly disciplined party. It is a vehicle of collective demands that can no longer be satisfied through the traditional patron-client networks. The ideology of the party (both nationalist and socialist) is committed to a radical restructuring of the economy and society through nationalization and state intervention. Socialism brought together most of the underprivileged groups and if the economy grows it may attract the workers. But PASOK is also attractive to the more enlightened groups among the middle classes and the intelligentsia. Nationalism now appeals to them, too, especially when cast in terms of national independence and an end to foreign tutelage. Naturally, it also appeals to most of the traditionalist forces and the army.

The election also amounted to a critical redistribution of political power, and ultimately of economic and social power, through the participation of new groups among the urban dwellers and the neutralization, for the time being at least, of others. Consequently, PASOK both represents and symbolizes a new political synthesis—national, consensual, and participatory—that supersedes the previous one. Like the Democratic sweep in the United States in 1936 and the Gaullists' victory in 1962, the election of 1981 in Greece amounted to a genuine realignment of political forces, foreshadowing a new political era.

This in a nutshell is the argument according to which the election was a critical one—*pace*, Dean Burnham.

A Protest Vote

There is a protest vote, as opposed to a critical election, when the shift among voters from one party to another is not attributable to shifts among important constituent groups that share compatible ideological perceptions and policy objectives. It is ephemeral and episodic, inherently unstructured and unstable. In these terms, a case can be also made that the Greek election of 1981 was a protest vote.

The electoral figures indicated a massive transfer of votes from center-right to PASOK. Some voters from the middle classes were attracted to PASOK by its reformist social and economic ideology and programs; others because of its nationalist appeal; still others simply because Nea Democratia deprived them of the normal spoils of political power or because they disliked its leaders. Some remained attached to the Atlantic Alliance and the Common Market while others were opposed to both. For some, the appeal of nationalism was primarily a national affirmation against the Turkish danger and even the Turkish presence in Cyprus; for others, it went so far as to amount to an endorsement of a new nonaligned status. Similarly, the voters who shifted from Nea Democratia to PASOK did so for nationalist reasons that went even beyond the wishes of many of the centrists. They favored a more pronounced affirmation of national power and independence against Turkey, against the United States, and (especially among many traditionalists) vis-à-vis Europe. It reflected the hardest core of Greek nationalism—the reassertion of the identity of a Christian-Greek culture against the outside world. It was a nationalism with strong populist and authoritarian overtones that attracted many among those who had supported the military junta. Many in the army, among the junior officers, and in the lower clergy shared this nationalist outlook. But in contrast, as we already noted, some of the more enlightened groups both in the center and on the right—engineers, civil servants, academics, and educators —saw in Papandreou the embodiment of Western technocratic ideas. The Greek technocrats shifted to PASOK with the hope that they would participate in a social engineering task of economic development that best suited Greece's needs. Nationalism is not only the last refuge of a scoundrel, as has been said; it also makes strange bedfellows among the virtuous. This was the case for many of the groups from the center and the right that voted for PASOK.

Socialism—the second plank in the PASOK program—appealed for diverse reasons to many different groups, some of them workers, students, intellectuals, the poor, and the marginals. But it was also rejected by many who voted for PASOK. This was notably true of many in the middle classes, the lower middle classes, and the peasantry. Previous surveys indicated that a good proportion of PASOK voters did not take PASOK's socialist platform seriously.[2] They simply thought of it as campaign verbiage designed to attract the left or deter many from voting for the communist party. Andreas Papandreou was often viewed in terms of his father, for whom socialism was an alien thought. An appreciable group gave its support reluctantly, only when Mitterrand won the election in France and Papandreou appeared as a Mitterrand Socialist. In overall terms, there was no a priori reason to oppose state control and state ownership in a country that since 1974 and even before had, like France under the Gaullists, put investment, banking, and transportation under state regulation and control. State controls and state direction of the economy appealed to many in Greece, as in France, for national and nationalist reasons. Thus socialism attracted a number of voters but left others completely indifferent, incredulous, or downright hostile.

Socialism, however, is one thing; socialism with various popular and functional participatory mechanisms, together with decentralization of the state apparatus, is another. It does not appeal to many. Civil servants and technocrats object to it; farmers are attached deeply to their own plots; there has been no past practice of communal ownership in Greece, as there has been, for instance, in Yugoslavia. The workers may be unwilling to manage their own factories and blur class lines. The petite bourgeoisie, the great number of people employed in services, and individual workers and artisans do not comprehend it. If a Socialist system were ever to be put into operation, it would have to be run by a strong political party—PASOK and its militants— and become more authoritarian in substance than democratic and participatory. As a result, it could alienate many of the PASOK voters who never took the prospect of socialism seriously.

There are groups that wavered prior to the election and tilted in the direction of PASOK: the army, the lower clergy, the intelligentsia, and the university students. Their members and voters are likely to reconsider their vote. The first two may shape their attitudes in response to Papandreou's nationalist stance and the degree of his intransigence vis-à-vis Turkey. Here, international constraints may limit Papandreou's ardor and undermine his popularity. If not, Papandreou's stance may provoke powerful and humiliating responses from Turkey and again this may discourage many of his nationalist supporters. As for the intelligentsia and the university students, the problem of job opportunities may become more important than ideology. Some, however, will want to see Papandreou implement his socialist and foreign policy pledges as rapidly as possible. This segment of the radicalized university youth and intelligentsia will push for the realization of extreme solutions.

Finally, there is the problem of PASOK's leadership. The organization and structure, the discipline, and the mass membership of this new party stem from and depend on its leader. PASOK, like most protest movements, is a leader party. When in opposition, a protest movement always rides on the crest of its criticisms and the multiple and often contradictory "antis" of its ideology. But if it does not manage to silence criticism when in government, it may become the victim of its own electoral success and the aspirations it engendered. Any weakening of the leader's image amounts to a weakening of the party and of the symbols that hold its various parts and its voters together. There is no reason to believe at this stage that the structure and organization of the party will manage to produce a new leadership, in case of Papandreou's default. If the charisma of the leader wanes, the multiple voices of protest that united behind him may degenerate into a tower of Babel.

In conclusion, according to this argument, it is unlikely that the shift in votes in 1981 will translate itself into a stable realignment of political forces. Support from traditionalists and right-wingers may not last. There may be a split between the liberal reformist and the socialist-inspired voters of PASOK. The split may occur over economic and social policy and may become apparent only when economic problems mount. It is also likely that the nationalist component and the socialist component of PASOK's program will appear irreconcilable. The alliance may break between the forces attracted to PASOK because of its nationalist program and those attracted by its populist catchall pledges to as many segments and groups and interests as possible.

Equally relevant are the conflicts likely to develop over foreign policy among the liberal centrists who voted for PASOK. An extreme nationalist policy that confronts Turkey and a continuing strong anti-Atlantic or anti-European stance may alienate many. Economic difficulties and added burdens on the middle classes may alienate all of them. If the prices of agricultural products decline, if inflation and the trade deficit mount, if unemployment grows, the shoe will be on the other foot. The decline may well be attributed by many to Papandreou's economic policies. It will be very easy, under such conditions, to see a reversal in the votes and support of the peasantry and the lower middle class.

PASOK's protest against virtually all aspects of the Greek system and of the political synthesis since 1946 carried powerful revolutionary implications, appealed to incompatible groups, reached out to contradictory forces and ideologies, and challenged and endangered many powerful foreign interests. The political forces marshaled by PASOK in the election of 1981 are so contradictory and incompatible that they are unlikely to remain together and continue to give their support to it.

This in a nutshell is the argument that the 1981 election was a protest vote.

The Municipal Election of October 1982

The arguments favoring the protest vote thesis are strengthened by the outcome of the municipal election of October 1982 in which PASOK lost some 7–9 percent of its strength in such major urban centers as Athens, Salonica, and Chania. Both the communist party to the left and Nea Democratia to the center-right gained, at PASOK's expense, on the first ballot (see Table 3). PASOK's left-wing constituency showed its dissatisfaction with the nonfulfillment of many electoral pledges both in the economy and in foreign policy, while some middle-class supporters began to resent higher taxes and added social charges. PASOK was, of course, victorious on the second ballot (which took place when no candidate received more than 50 percent of the votes on the first), thanks to the support of the communists and often their direct cooperation. PASOK won the great majority of the municipalities. However, where the second balloting was limited to a contest between a PASOK and a communist candidate, especially in some urban centers, it was the communist candidate who won because of the defection of PASOK voters. It appeared that the shifting and precarious coalition of forces that rallied behind PASOK in 1981 was beginning to break.

Serious questions can also be raised, but without survey work cannot be clearly answered, about two related issues: the extent of communist penetration of PASOK among voters and within the party and the prospects of communist support for PASOK in future elections.

There is no doubt about growing communist strength among voters. The major losses of PASOK in the municipal elections resulted in major gains for the Communists. The inference is clear: a good proportion of PASOK voters in 1981 were close to the KKE. In 1981 they voted for PASOK because they feared that a vote for the Communists would have been wasted. "Votez utile" meant a vote for Mitterrand in France. It also meant a vote for PASOK in Greece. This was not the case, however, in the municipal elections. In 1982

Table 3

1982 MUNICIPAL ELECTION RESULTS IN SOME MAJOR CITIES

	PASOK	Nea Democratia	Communists
Athens	−9.18	+3.54	+5.91
Salonica	−14.38	+5.24	+12.35
Rhodes	−15.09	+2.18	−
Tripoli	−5.3	+8.06	−
Larissa	−13.43	+0.34	+15.48
Tricalla	−8.79	−	+14.72
Chania	−15.14	−	+14.56
Patras	−	−	−
Sparta	−6.86	−7.30	−
Florina	−5.9	−8.69	−
Kavalla	−14.04	−	+9.65

SOURCE: *Epikentra* 28 (September-October 1982) Athens.

many of the PASOK voters were also reacting against the broken electoral promises of PASOK.

It is more difficult to ascertain the extent of the KKE's organizational penetration of PASOK. In municipalities where the second ballot pitted PASOK against the KKE, the organizational drive of the first was neutralized by communist militants. Organizational penetration was effective in every municipality and town where the Leftist Front—a list consisting of PASOK, Communists, and some others—won. Communist municipal councillors will make their weight and their discipline felt in the municipal councils. In fact, if the PASOK leadership were to falter, the administration of over 143 towns where the Front won will be even more vulnerable to communist penetration and even control.

As for the electoral support that the Communists provided to PASOK, the figures give us the most eloquent answer: on the first round of the municipal election PASOK won in 21 towns, the Communists in 10, Nea Democratia in 39, and the Leftist Front in 65. On the second ballot, the Front (mostly with PASOK candidates as mayors) won in 142, PASOK alone in 15, the Communists in 28, and Nea Democratia in 17.

The overall conclusion from the results of the municipal elections seems inescapable. If legislative elections were to be held under the present electoral system, PASOK could not get a majority in the *Vouli*. To get one, or in order to form a government, PASOK would have to seek the cooperation of the communist party, either before the elections in the form of reciprocal voting arrangements and alliances or in the *Vouli* with a coalition cabinet in which Communists participate. Thus the communist party becomes, only ten years after it was legalized, a very important factor in our assessment of future developments.

The Communist Factor

Before World War II, the Communist Party of Greece (KKE) occupied a marginal place in Greek politics. It displayed the same characteristics as all communist parties, subservience to the Third International—that is, to Moscow—and a solid organization and discipline. It enjoyed the support of workers in the urban areas. As almost everywhere in Western Europe, its political take-off came with the invasion of Russia by Hitler's forces. Like the communist parties in France and Italy, the KKE played a key part in the organization of a national resistance (1941–1944), in which it assumed a predominant political role. It controlled the major guerrilla organization (ELAS), a well-organized and well-armed force (thanks to Italian weapons) that by 1944 dominated the whole country. In December 1944, ELAS attempted to gain political power but was thwarted by the arrival of British forces in Athens. The communist-led guerrilla forces made a desperate bid for power in the Civil War (1946–1949), which was gradually localized in Epirus, close to Albania and Yugoslavia. The rebel forces showed a remarkable tenacity, organization, and ruthlessness but massive American aid to the government forces denied them their goal—the seizure of political power.

The Civil War left bitter memories of division. For the Communists and their sympathizers it was a historic opportunity that was lost.[3] For their opponents, it was an event that should not be allowed to recur. The very fact that American aid accounted for the defeat of the communist-led forces left some with a blind loyalty to Moscow, while from others it elicited an equally blind pro-American stance. The Communists bided their time—and Communists know how. Despite the decades of repression that followed the Civil War during which the party was outlawed and the long period during which the Communists or communist sympathizers were systematically purged from all public and often private services, the hard core of the communist party maintained its organization and kept its vision alive.

The beginning of the "third round"—their third opportunity after the Resistance and the Civil War—came in 1974. The party was legalized and surprisingly won almost 10 percent of the vote, with about 2 percent going to what has become known as the Communist Party of the Interior (KKE-I), a Eurocommunist group that split from the pro-Soviet leadership of the KKE. The Communists first tried to mend their fences. They proclaimed their democratic profession of faith and appeared reformist at home but advocated a foreign policy that was in all respects identical to that of the Soviet Union. They also asserted their unqualified nationalism and a commitment to national independence that was now directed against Turkey and the United States. They asked for withdrawal from NATO and the closing of the American (NATO) bases, and they had no patience with any European entanglements. They appealed to their traditional constituencies, where they continued to have an underground network of contacts, and began to infiltrate municipalities and develop strength in the universities among students and intellectuals, while maintaining their hold over working-class groups in the urban areas.

PASOK appeared both as an enemy and a friend and the *amici-enemici* complex unfolded in its usual way. It is still in the process of deepening and growing. PASOK as a self-professed Marxist party, but also nationalist and anti-American, threatened the communist ascendancy on the left—and it was without any doubt Papandreou's intent to do just that. But it also legitimized the communist party and its foreign policy goals. PASOK leadership agreed that the KKE was a "democratic force," a "progressive factor," and a bona fide "vehicle of *Allaghi*" (Change). The heroes of the Resistance were once more praised and the Civil War forgotten and forgiven. The Communists jumped on the bandwagon offered to them and while maintaining their distance from PASOK—they honestly doubted the revolutionary credentials of PASOK and its leader—were eager to benefit from the semblance of left-wing unity. They questioned PASOK's claim to alone represent the left and insisted that only the cooperation of the two "brother parties" could ensure socialism and democracy and bring about *Allaghi*. They offered support and cooperation and even hinted at participating in the government.

While PASOK and the KKE were in opposition until 1981, only matters of emphasis separated them. The KKE appeared more moderate in matters of social and economic change. It was just as hostile to NATO, the Common Market, and the American bases, and its anti-Turkish stance put them among the ranks of all good patriots. There were obvious frictions. The Communists in their electoral campaign appealed to the electorate, asking for at least 17 percent of the vote. This would have given them a sizable number of seats in the *Vouli* and would have stopped PASOK from gaining a majority and forming a government alone. With such strength they would have been able to put pressure on PASOK, discredit it, infiltrate its local and regional organization, and attract many of its left-wing voters and militants. They failed, getting about 11 percent of the vote. Was the party frozen to this percentage? It is doubtful.

The Communists' strength was revealed in the municipal election of October 1982, one year after the legislative elections, a year in which Papandreou and PASOK were the government. The KKE spelled out its overall future strategy and it is quite likely that, unless there are significant shifts in the present position of PASOK, they will adhere to it in the forthcoming elections. The communist party stayed clearly to the left, admonishing PASOK for its halfhearted reforms, its unwillingness to proceed rapidly with decentralization, and its reluctance to proceed with truly structural changes in the economy and society. *Allaghi* remained at the level of rhetoric. The KKE sternly admonished the government for turning its back on its electoral pledges with regard to NATO, the Common Market, and the American bases and continued to agitate and to organize demonstrations against what it termed "Amerikanocratia." As economic conditions worsened and unemployment rose steadily, the KKE reached out to the workers and artisans and to the mass of the new city dwellers for support.

The communist party was becoming PASOK's mentor but also a permanent source and organizer of agitation at its left flank. True *Allaghi* could not be accomplished without its cooperation. The KKE reversed the situation that existed before the election when Papandreou had stolen its left-wing semi-revolutionary populist thunder and especially its nationalism and anti-Americanism. The KKE now was claiming to be the only party that would strive for the integrity and independence of the country, which was synonymous with liberating it from American imperialism and domination. PASOK, though a positive force, could not be relied upon to accomplish this, certainly not alone. Particular attention was paid to the need for genuine decentralization, to allow the periphery initiative and self-government. The election of communist mayors would guarantee honest local administration, for the Communists, the KKE leadership claimed, had proven themselves honest, energetic, and efficient administrators, putting the interest of the collectivity above personal and party considerations.

The Communists' strategy and electoral tactics paid off, as indicated in the survey of municipal elections. In most urban centers, the KKE did better than the 17 percent goal they had set for themselves in the legislative election a year before. The party became for the first time in Greek political history an electoral force that counts. The moment it can win 20 percent of the voters its friendship toward PASOK may undergo a profound change. At the present, in terms of the party line outlined in the report of the Central Committee before the 11th Party Congress held in December 1982 and endorsed by it, KKE will cooperate with PASOK at the mass level and try to erase anticommunist prejudices among the followers of PASOK. It will seek to attract all those who are not satisfied with the government and continue to advocate a real *Allaghi* while blaming PASOK for failing to live up to its electoral pledges—domestic and foreign. The KKE reserved to itself the right to continue to critically evaluate the policies of the socialist government. Indeed, it promised to undertake a "constructive criticism" in hopes of bringing new members and militants to the party but without formulating explicitly any demands to participate in the government. On the contrary, the KKE promises to be at the forefront of the class struggle and assume responsibilities only in a genuine people's democracy. The secretary-general noted, however, the common positions of his party and PASOK with regard to monopolistic and foreign capitalism and imperialism, and he pointed to the existence of a "common language" between the two parties. He warned the congress of hasty and inconsiderate criticisms against PASOK, despite the latter's "hegemonical" tendencies. He felt sure that the Communists would be able to show with concrete actions their attachment to the common goals that unite the left.

In short, the strategy of the communist party is to maintain and enhance its legitimacy; to reinforce it with a renewed emphasis on its past efforts and sacrifices and the patriotism it displayed in the years of the Resistance and Civil War when the enemy was essentially the same as now; to strengthen its organization and membership; to infiltrate various municipalities everywhere; and to wait until PASOK weakens or the leader falters. "He who waits, hunts best."

6 | Current Trends

After two years in office the government's record ought to provide us with some answers to the question we raised: is it a bona fide socialist government in the tradition of Western socialism or is it moving in the direction of Third World authoritarian socialism? Is its populist phase about to give way to regime consolidation and statism? There are at least three basic considerations in terms of which we can evaluate the record of the government and the present course of the Greek socialist movement: (1) have the government and PASOK shown respect for pluralism or are they moving in the direction of authoritarianism; (2) have the party and the leader increased their popularity or are they losing it; (3) is the populist phase of the PASOK election as strong as ever or is there a noticeable trend away from it and in the direction of statism?

The Government in Flux

There has been thus far a great disparity between the ongoing rhetoric and the achievements of the government. The party and often its leader, the prime minister, continue to state their goals in messianic terms: an end to exploitation, the control of the economy by the state and the people, and national independence. They declare that *Allaghi* is irreversible and that it constitutes the last stop on the way to full democracy. They continue to emphasize that without the people's participation, control, and decision making, socialism and economic development cannot be realized. They appeal to all non-privileged Greeks for support. Similarly, despite numerous zigzags, the rhetoric remains anti-NATO, anti-American, and, in substance, anti-Western. Some affinities have been noted with the French Socialists, especially with regard to their domestic reforms—notably decentralization. Membership in the Common Market seems to have been accepted, at least as long as Greece receives special treatment and benefits. These amounted to about $800 million in 1981–1982 and Greece was expected to receive $1.6 billion from the European Investment Bank in 1983.

Powerful political considerations at home made it difficult for the government either to carry out its pledges with regard to NATO—to withdraw and remove the American bases—or to negotiate in good faith the terms of its continuing participation in NATO and the terms under which the American bases will be maintained. The reasons were quite simple: if the government signed an agreement on the bases then it would lose many of its left-wing militants and lay itself open to challenge by the KKE. If Greece withdrew from NATO and cancelled the agreement on the bases, it might lose American and even Common Market economic and political support without which the economy cannot survive. It would also lose support from the moderate part of its electorate.

In July 1983, after lengthy negotiations, a new five-year agreement to maintain the U.S. bases in Greece was signed. Papandreou presented the agreement as a termination of Greek dependence, claiming that the bases would be removed within the period covered by the agreement upon request of the Greek government. Speaking to the Central Committee of PASOK right after the agreement had been concluded, he referred to it as a "historic agreement for the removal of the United States' bases from Greece." It signaled the beginning of Greek independence. He reiterated that Greece would follow its own foreign policy and strategy. In this manner, he tried to appease both his left and the Communists, who demanded the immediate withdrawal of the bases, and PASOK's centrist and moderate followers, who favored the continuation of the bases. But he was apparently unsuccessful. The first group saw in the new agreement a continuation of past policies and a flagrant breach of Papandreou's electoral pledges; the second found Papandreou's remarks about termination premature and misleading.

With regard to Poland, Afghanistan, the Middle East, the denuclearization of the Balkans that the prime minister advocates, and the deployment of Pershing missiles in Europe, the government has taken a clearly anti-American and often a pro-Soviet stance. It is a stand that neutralizes the communist party to its left and many of the communist sympathizers in PASOK, but antagonizes its moderate supporters.

This ambivalence is likely to continue. It is both divisive and explosive, because in the last analysis, reality may yield to ideology. But it is also potentially divisive. Any decision on NATO and the bases will drive a wedge between the left-wing and the moderate elements of PASOK, moving the former to the communist party and the latter to Nea Democratia. On the other hand, no firm decision at all may progressively undermine support for PASOK, both from the left and the center-right.

Thus the government's record on foreign policy is clearly uncertain. The Common Market has been accepted tentatively and cautiously as long as the rich nations pay and as long as they let Greece maintain a special status. Relations with Turkey alternate between dialogue and confrontation, and while the Cypriot Greeks continue to be defended there has been no progress in the settlement of the intra-Cyprus dispute between Greeks and Turks—another source of Greek-Turkish conflict that may erupt or be exploited at any time. Nor have solicitations to the Soviets brought about any changes in the Greek international or economic situation. Similarly, relations with the Arab nations and a continuing anti-Israel and pro-PLO posture have brought no commercial or trade benefits to Greece.

The record of the government shows the same ambivalence in its domestic program. There is the same discrepancy between rhetoric and accomplishment. The record is positive with regard to some long-overdue liberal reforms: civil marriage, divorce, the separation between church and state, abolition of the venerable institution of the dowry, and the lifting of criminal penalties for adultery that victimized women. The same is true with regard to some welfare measures: retirement and health benefits have been raised and expanded to include women on the farm. Social security benefits for unemployment and sickness have been extended to farmers and agricultural laborers. Wages have been raised and so have the salaries of civil servants and army personnel, but the increases have only matched the inflation that continues to hover at around 20 percent a year.

In contrast there have been few, if any, major structural reforms of the economy or the society. No new nationalization has taken place, simply because the major enterprises in energy, transportation, telecommunications, banking, and aviation already belonged to the public sector and are operated by state agencies. Most private industrial concerns in Greece are small. Private investment has been negligible; it usually comes through low-interest loans from the banks, which are controlled by the state. The rhetoric favoring nationalization, in other words, was only the reassertion of a principle.

In agriculture, farmers' cooperatives have been promoted to cut down the profits of middlemen and to keep prices down. They seem to have been successful among the olive farmers but less so with the producers of vegetables and fruit. However, EEC subsidies to olive oil producers have been the reason for success. Among farmers with larger holdings such as in cereals and tobacco, cooperatives have not been successfully organized as yet.

The most important economic activity—shipping—continues to elude the government simply because most Greek-owned ships are registered outside of Greece. Legislation has been enacted providing for better working conditions for seamen on ships flying the Greek flag and for a "hire-Greeks" policy.

All in all, while *Allaghi* remains the motto of the party, there have been few *allaghes* (changes) in the society and the economy. And little has been done to alleviate some of Greece's major predicaments; pollution remains rampant, especially in Athens, and the Socialists have failed to whisk away the smog that hangs over most of Attica, as they had promised. Inflation seems to have dropped by about 2–3 percent and now averages 20 percent. But unemployment, which was insignificant in 1979–80, has risen to about 10 percent; investments are down and the trade deficit continues to rise. Without massive loans and subsidies from the Common Market and without tourism, the Greek economy would be in a far more difficult situation. The government is beginning to reconsider its policies and to favor austerity measures and increases in productivity, following the Mitterrand example.

The government seems also to have failed to promote grass-roots socialism, the equivalent of the French *autogestion* or of the municipal socialism of older vintage. Towns and municipalities have been encouraged to start and run their own enterprises and about 8 percent of budgeted expenditures will be distributed in various ways to the municipalities that launch new ones. The grant cannot exceed 50 percent of the total investment. The plan, however, does not seem to have worked as yet. Many municipalities do not have adequate resources to match the government grant; others do not have the personnel; others are in the dark about the specific arrangements proposed and do not know what will happen if the business or the enterprise they undertake goes bankrupt. Municipal socialism is suspect because the large government corporations in gas, communications, electricity, and transportation are deeply in debt. Ideological reasons prevent the launching of new enterprises, especially in municipalities under either the control or the influence of the Communists, since they involve business incentives and profit. However, the opportunity to secure funds directly from the government will be welcome to many and the possibility that they will be solicited and granted for political purposes is very likely. Given the fact that two-thirds of all municipalities and towns are in the hands of the Communists or PASOK or are held by a PASOK-communist majority, municipal socialism may be used to build a solid network of political controls and loyalties far more reliable and cohesive than the old patron-client arrangements.

The Role of the Party

The real content of socialism in Greece, unlike Western socialism, can be detected in the growing politicization of the economy, social services, and public and governmental services, including civil service, health services, the media, and education. Again, only trends can be detected. But the overall picture is that of a concerted effort to purge and control the public services at the top while infiltrating and controlling the local bodies. The major mechanism used is the party; various PASOK groups (they are called "branches") in virtually all public, social, and economic organizations check on the political orthodoxy of civil servants, educators, hospital personnel, public corporation executives, and bankers and pass on new appointments. They are active in all public corporations, from Olympic Airlines to the Greek Tourist Office, and in the universities, the banks, and the hospitals.

Outright dismissals and a policy of early retirement have been used to purge many top civil servants and provide for patronage to supporters—a common phenomenon not peculiar only to Greek politics. But it is the constant surveillance by the party cadres that is novel. It is not limited to appointments or promotions but often extends to government deliberations and decisions. It is not restricted to the public sector but also affects private institutions and the universities that by law and tradition are totally independent from state interference. In the civil service, replacements have come from among the believers. In the universities, new legislation gives far too much power to student organizations that are controlled by the Communists and PASOK. Television and most newspapers owe their existence to government subsidies and loans and face a difficult future unless they toe the government line. The great majority of them favor the government. So does the publicly controlled television, whose neutrality had never been assured in Greece.

In short, the contours of socialism can be defined in terms of PASOK's growing political control. The party has infiltrated and occasionally supplanted the decision-making organs, and in so doing the leadership is building integrative mechanisms of political control. PASOK continues to be strong and well-organized, operating under the principles and practices of democratic centralism, allowing no factions or dissidence within its ranks. It continues to be particularly active in the countryside and among the young. It now has over 170,000 members. However, after two years the party has not managed to destroy or to absorb oppositional groups. On the contrary, the KKE is gaining, both organizationally and electorally, and the opposition party, the Nea Democratia, made an unexpected electoral comeback in the municipal elections of 1982. Only the center seems to have disappeared, at least for the time being.

Despite, or perhaps because of, the ubiquitousness of the party, frictions have developed between it and state personnel, including the ministers. There is an ambiguity as to the respective roles of the state and the party. The former is supposed to make and implement decisions, the latter to mobilize support and formulate the main policy options to be presented to the electorate. There is every indication, however, that the party and the leader continue to overshadow and control the state and the government services.

Within the party the leader has strengthened his control. Nominations to regional and local units require his endorsement. He is free (and has exercised this freedom) to dismiss members at the slightest sign of dissidence. Debate in the party congresses is structured in advance and there has been no sign of any current other than the one imposed by the leadership. There are conflicts at the top and there are personal factions and cliques, some of them directed against Papandreou. But as yet they have not engendered serious factional conflicts that affect the rank and file.

The party overshadows its parliamentary representatives, who are expected to follow the line set by the party congresses and the directions of the leader. The role of the latter has been strengthened by a change in the electoral system abolishing preferential voting. The order of preference on the party ballot is now set by the leader himself and the voter cannot modify it. As a result, the leader's control over PASOK deputies will be futher tightened.

PASOK does not have the militancy of the KKE; nor is its discipline as tight. Yet with a larger membership and with government favors available to its militants and local representatives, it constitutes a powerful mass movement. Constant flirtation at the base, however, between PASOK and KKE members raises serious doubts about the loyalty of the former in one of the most sensitive areas of political and electoral action and mobilization— voting.

Regime Consolidation: The Statist Temptation

PASOK's ideology alternates between the old populist slogans of nationalism and *Allaghi* and the requirements of upholding the authority of the state and the needs of regime consolidation. It continues to walk the tightrope of populist slogans, scientific Marxism, utopian socialism, Swedish welfarism, modernization and industrialization under state control, and Greek-Christian nationalism. But a pragmatic outlook, a professional elitism, and a nationalism qualified by considerations of maintaining power surface not too infrequently. The Common Market seems to have been accepted; the U.S. bases will remain for at least five years; the many dialogues with the Turks have not been interrupted; the status quo in Cyprus has been maintained.

There has been increasing concern with technical considerations, not the least of which is the procurement of capital from the West. It is a need that comes into conflict with the frequent romantic challenges to the West and the United States. Economic planning and controls have become necessary, along with postponement of the fulfillment of promises made to consumers. The leader was forced to seek out managers rather than politicians.

There have also been noticeable trends away from populism. Efforts are being made to strengthen some nonparty institutions. The state, the bureaucracy, and PASOK loyalists are vying for control. Pledges about decentralization notwithstanding, local and regional representative bodies are coming more and more under the control of the central government. Party government, according to some, may be losing out to the requirements of statism.

Many managers and technocrats are becoming impatient with rhetoric and delays. They advocate austerity measures that inevitably invite popular dissatisfaction and unrest. The only answer lies in the adoption of control measures. The state and its bureaucracy may become the instrument of planning and control, while the party may only propagate the new doctrines of the leader and legitimize his control. Modernization and economic growth may necessitate state authoritarianism, in which the army may have to play a strong supporting role. As in many Third World countries, but unlike Western European societies, Greek socialism may move from populism to authoritarianism. The constraints and the obstacles are many, but the temptations and opportunities are even greater.

Populist rhetoric won the election for PASOK in 1981. But such rhetoric cannot be reconciled with a stable economic policy and regime maintenance that call for investment and therefore heavy borrowing from abroad and an austerity program at home that includes freezing public spending, prices, and wages. Papandreou may have to turn his back to many demands and insist on austerity while he seeks credits from the international money markets. He may have to subordinate the ideology and rhetoric of PASOK, even detach himself from his own party and find other ways to structure his leadership and institutionalize his charisma—in other words, establish a personal government. Already the establishment of his own personal bureau (the Cabinet of the Prime Minister), legislation that gives him the right to have his candidates on the PASOK list elected in the order of his preference, and the diminished role of PASOK members in the *Vouli* (they are gradually to lose all initiative in the preparation and the enactment of legislation) are all significant steps in the direction of personal government.

The results of the municipal elections strengthened the statist temptation. They showed that the PASOK electorate, and perhaps a good percentage of PASOK members, lean toward the Communists while others may turn toward the center or Nea Democratia. If modernization is to go on unhindered, the demands that continue to cry out for satisfaction, backed by the leadership of a strong communist party, will have to be controlled and silenced. It will not be the first time that a self-professed Marxist turned against a communist party, and Papandreou may not be the last to do so.

Electoral Support

There has been a decline of electoral support for PASOK. The middle classes are beginning to reconsider their position. The liberal reforms mentioned earlier satisfied many. However, others have been disenchanted by higher taxation, the devaluation of the drachma, the lack of adequate investment opportunities, the priorities given to the public sector and to public enterprises, the failure to deal with some of the most malignant forms of pollution and urban transportation (particularly in Athens) and the uncertainties of Greek foreign policy and defense.

The farmers continue to support PASOK, primarily because of the benefits accruing to them from Common Market subsidies that they attribute to PASOK. Their continuing support will depend therefore in great part on the future agricultural policy of the Common Market. It will also depend on the scope and the specific policies of farmers' cooperatives. The slightest interference with private property rights will provoke an adverse reaction. The workers, on the other hand, appear to follow the KKE. Efforts by the government to interfere with trade unions and to qualify the right to strike, through some of the legislative measures passed, will intensify their protest and opposition. So will austerity measures.

But in the last analysis, neither the farmers nor the workers will be the decisive force. It is the large and rather amorphous lower middle class that will play the critical role. It comprises school teachers, clerical personnel, low echelon civil service employees, small shop owners, and the large numbers of those who work in the tertiary sector, particularly in the tourist industry. They benefited from some of the early welfare measures passed by the government but ongoing inflation has nullified some of these benefits while unemployment is adversely affecting many in this group. It is a particularly volatile group; as we noted, many of them have moved from their villages to the urban centers over the past 30 years. They are losing their roots without managing to plant new ones. Many of the second generation attend the university—a center of agitation and radicalization. It is this large group that is particularly sensitive to populist slogans. Unlike the lower middle classes in advanced capitalist societies that have strong affinities with the middle classes, they find themselves socially and ideologically closer to the workers and farmers. Hostility to the establishment unites them, and uncertainties about occupation and status make them receptive to extremist solutions. While it appears that PASOK is still holding on to their support, it is growing more conditional and uncertain.

7 | Conclusion

No clear answer can be given as yet to the question we asked at the very beginning of this study: What course will Greek socialism follow?

In contrast to Western Europe, socialism is new in Greece. After 1920, the Greek communist party preempted the very small working class, some artisans' groups, a fraction of the intelligentsia, and above all the ideology of revolution and socialism. Self-styled agrarian Socialists addressed themselves primarily to the farmers, advocating land redistribution, formation of cooperatives, agrarian banks to provide low-interest loans, and other measures. In other words, we do not have the proper historical perspective to pass judgment on PASOK's political and ideological heritage. It is only about ten years old.

Despite the unavoidable disparity between rhetoric and action, however, certain characteristics are apparent.

1. PASOK continues to claim to be a Marxist party.
2. Nonetheless, PASOK does not claim to be a class party but rather appeals broadly across classes—to all nonprivileged Greeks. It distinguishes sharply between the "establishment" and "the people."
3. PASOK's leader and founder played a predominant role in fashioning PASOK. It is a leader party.
4. *Allaghi* (Change) expresses the sum of many populist pledges: radical structural reforms of the economy and the society, fundamental redistribution of welfare measures, and a major reorientation of Greek foreign policy.

5. PASOK made sweeping populist pledges with regard to the people's participation in government. It promised administrative decentralization and direct popular government through people's committees.

6. This populism merged with equally powerful nationalist themes against NATO, Turkey, and the Common Market. Nationalism and nationalist themes relating to Turkey have always had a powerful mobilizing effect in Greece and were just as much a mobilizing ideology as PASOK's egalitarian and anti-establishment populist slogans.

In contrast to the socialist parties of the Third World, however, PASOK and the pronouncements of its leader appeared to remain within the tradition of Western socialism by promising political pluralism. Despite his strong showing at the polls in 1981, PASOK's leader restated his belief in the freedom and the rights of the opposition. Yet PASOK's promises to maintain democracy and the democratic attachment of its leader have not been seriously tested as yet. It is not tolerance of opposition in the abstract that counts, but tolerance when the opposition becomes a threat. Many one-party Third World socialist regimes also endorse the idea of pluralism if it finds expression within the party. Subtle theories about conflictless pluralism within one party have been developed by Chinese and African socialist leaders, including Moammar Khadafy, while conflictual pluralism has been singled out as detrimental to national unity and independence.

If socialism is new in Greece, authoritarianism is very much a part of the political tradition of the country. Military authoritarian regimes have come and gone. Statist-bureaucratic authoritarianism describes accurately the fascist regime of 1936–1941 under Joannes Metaxas. It was a regime that relied upon the monarchy, the bureaucracy, the police, the higher clergy, business groups, including a sizable part of the middle classes, and, of course, the military. Like Franquismo, it did not develop a strong party or generate an ideology. Greece has never experienced an authoritarian regime based on a single party, and PASOK appears to be the only mass party capable of providing the organization and the support to sustain such an authoritarian government.

The temptation of authoritarian socialism remains great; many of the trends we noted in the direction of party control and the increasingly dominant position of the leader indicate that authoritarianism is the most likely course that will be followed. Whether it takes the form of one-party socialism or state socialism or a combination of the two is difficult to say. The ultimate choice between the two models of authoritarian socialism—party or state—will depend on particular political circumstances as they develop. The most significant will be the charisma and popularity of PASOK's leader, economic conditions, the strength and tactics of the communist party, and, most unpredictable of all, the international situation in the southeast Mediterranean.

It should be clearly noted that there is one overpowering and unifying theme, nationalism, to which PASOK mainly owes its victory. Any incident in any of the hundreds of the Aegean islands, over the disputed airspace of the Aegean, or in Cyprus, whether real or imaginary, accidental or contrived, can unleash it. The Greeks do not have to search the map to find their Falkland Islands. A strong nationalist stance will unite them all behind the party and the leader and will not allow dissent or opposition. It will elicit the full patriotic support of the KKE, bring the middle classes back into the fold, and neutralize or dismantle Nea Democratia. It will still whatever waverings that might linger among the armed forces and will receive the blessings of the church.

Notes

Chapter 1

1. Juan Linz, "Europe's Southern Frontier: Evolving Trends Toward What?" *Daedalus* (Winter 1979): 175–209.

2. Samuel P. Huntington, *Political Order in Changing Societies* (New Haven: Yale University Press, 1968), particularly chap. 1.

3. The term was coined by Huntington to indicate rapid social change and mobilization of new groups on the one hand and slow development of political institutions on the other. It is a highly unstable situation in which regimes may change frequently.

4. The two best essays on the destabilizing effects of economic growth are Karl W. Deutsch, "Social Mobilization and Political Development," *American Political Science Review* 55, no. 3 (September 1961): 493–502; and Mancur Olson, Jr., "Rapid Growth as a Destabilizing Force," *The Journal of Economic History* 3, no. 4 (December 1963): 529–52.

Chapter 2

1. The most relevant studies of authoritarianism are Amos Perlmutter, *Modern Authoritarianism* (New Haven: Yale University Press, 1981); David Collier, ed., *The New Authoritarianism in Latin America* (Princeton: Princeton University Press, 1979); and Helen Desfosses and Jacques Levesque, eds., *Socialism in the Third World* (New York: Praeger, 1975), in which the socialist experiments in Chile, Cuba, Syria, Iraq, Libya, Algeria, Mali, Ghana, Tanzania, Sri Lanka, and Pakistan are reviewed. Also see Juan Linz, *The Breakdown of Democratic Regimes* (Baltimore: Johns Hopkins Press, 1980); Samuel P. Huntington and Clement Moore, *Authoritarian Politics in Modern Society* (New

York: Basic Books, 1970); and Guillermo O'Donnell, *Modernization and Bureaucratic Authoritarianism: Studies in Latin American Politics* (Berkeley: Institute of International Studies, University of California, 1973).

2. On democratic socialism, see R. H. S. Crossman, *The Politics of Socialism* (New York: Atheneum, 1965); Michael Harrington, *Socialism* (New York: Bantam Books, 1972); and W. E. Patterson and Ian Campbell, *Social Democracy in Post-War Europe* (New York: St. Martin's Press, 1974).

3. See the pioneering work of Gabriel Almond and Sidney Verba, *Civic Culture* (Princeton: Princeton University Press, 1958).

4. This is O'Donnell's major thesis in accounting for authoritarianism in Latin America. See also Collier, *The New Authoritarianism.*

5. For an overview of major Third World ideologies, see Paul E. Sigmund, ed., *Ideologies in Developing Nations* (New York: Praeger, 1972).

6. See Guillermo O'Donnell, "Tensions in the Bureaucratic-Authoritarian State and the Question of Democracy" and David Collier, "Overview of the Bureaucratic-Authoritarian Model" in Collier, *The New Authoritarianism.*

Chapter 3

1. In Jean Meynaud, *Les Forces politiques en Grèce* (Lausanne: Etudes de sciences politiques, 1964).

2. This is developed more fully in my "Democracy in Greece—For How Long?," *The Virginia Quarterly Review* 51, no. 4 (Autumn 1975): 531–550.

3. Giovanni Sartori, *Parties and Party Systems* (Cambridge, England: Cambridge University Press), particularly chap. 6.

4. For the elections of 1974 and 1977, see Howard Penniman, ed., *Greece at the Polls: 1974, 1977* (Washington, D.C.: American Enterprise Institute, 1979) pp. 16–17.

Chapter 4

1. For the PASOK program, see PASOK: *Diakirixi kyvernitikis politikis—Symvolaio me to lao* (Proclamation of a government program—covenant with the people) (Athens, Summer 1981); *The Government Program* (Greek Embassy, Washington, D.C., November 22, 1981); and the electoral pamphlets, Panhellenic Socialist Movement (PASOK), *Laos-PASOK stin exoussia kai tin Allaghi: to PASOK stin Kuvernissi—O Laos stin exoussia* (People and PASOK in command: PASOK in the government, the people in control) (Athens, 1981); and Communist Party of Greece (KKE), *Eklogiko Programma 1981* (Electoral program 1981) (Athens, 1981).

2. For the platform of the Nea Democratia, see *To Programma Tis Neas Democratias theti themelia Neas Epochis* (The program of Nea Democratia establishing the foundations of a new era) (Athens, 1981).

Chapter 5

1. Walter Dean Burnham, *Critical Elections and the Mainsprings of American Politics* (New York: W.W. Norton, 1970), p. 10.

2. In a survey poll for whose accuracy I cannot vouch, 28 percent of the voters considered themselves "liberal," 15 percent "conservative," and 15 percent "non-Marxist socialist." *Epikentra* (September-October 1981).

3. For a vivid account, see Nicholas Gage, *Eleni* (New York: Random House, 1981).

Suggested Readings

Alivizatos, Nikos C. *Les Constitutions politiques de la Grèce a travers les crises, 1922–1974*. Paris: Librairie de droit et de jurisprudence, 1979.

Campbell, John, and Sherrard, Philip. *Modern Greece*. London: Ernest Benn, 1968.

Clark-Carey, Jane P., and Carey, Andrew G. *The Web of Modern Greek Politics*. Cambridge, England: Cambridge University Press, 1968.

Clogg, R., and Yannopoulos, G. *Greece Under Military Rule*. London: Secker & Warburg, 1972.

Collier, David, ed. *The New Authoritarianism in Latin America*. Princeton: Princeton University Press, 1979.

Couloumbis, T.C., and Iatrides, J.O. *Greek-American Relations: A Critical Review*. New York: Pella, 1980.

Desfosses, Helen, and Levesque, Jacques, eds. *Socialism in the Third World*. New York: Praeger, 1975.

"Ekloges 1981: Deka Analyssis" (Ten analyses). *Politiki* (Political Science Review) (January-March 1982). Athens: Greek Political Science Association.

Epikentra (Center of Political Research and Information, Athens). See the analysis of the election results in no. 22 (September-October 1981); no. 28 (September-October 1982); no. 30 (January-February 1983).

Greece, House of Parliament. *The Constitution of Greece*. Athens, 1975.

Iatrides, John, ed. *Greece in the 1940s: A Nation in Crisis*. Hanover, N.H.: University Press of New England, 1981.

Legg, Keith R. *Politics in Modern Greece*. Stanford: Stanford University Press, 1969.

Linardatou, Spirou. *Synchoni Elliniki Istoria* (Contemporary Greek History). 4 vols. Athens: Papazissis, 1972–1981.

Meynaud, Jean. *Les Forces politiques en Grèce*. Lausanne: Etudes de sciences politiques, 1964.

Mouzelis, N. *Modern Greece: Facets of Underdevelopment*. London: Macmillan, 1978.

Penniman, Howard, ed. *Greece at the Polls: 1974, 1977*. Washington, D.C.: American Enterprise Institute, 1979.

Petras, J. "Greece: Democracy and Tanks," *Journal of the Hellenic Diaspora* 4 (1977): 3–30.

Poulantzas, N. *The Crisis of Dictatorship*. London: New Left Books, 1973.

Statistical Year Book of Greece, 1980. *Athens: National Statistical Service of Greece, 1980*.

Tsoucalas, Konstantinos. *The Greek Tragedy*. London: Penguin, 1969.

———. *Kinoniki Anaptixi kai Kratos: I Syngrotissi tou demossiou chorou tis Ellados* (Social development and the state: The organization of the public sector in Greece). Athens: Themelia, 1981.

———. "On the Problem of Political Clientelism in Greece in the Nineteenth Century." *Journal of Hellenic Diaspora* 5 (1978): 5–17.

Vatikiotis, P.J. *Greece: A Political Essay*. Beverly Hills, Calif.: Sage Publications, 1974.

HOOVER INTERNATIONAL STUDIES

DUE DATE

BU	NOV 2 9 1988		
	201-6503		Printed in USA